D1719165

LIVING
Legacy

Invest in **your community** while creating
significant **cash flow**

ISABELLE GUARINO

Copyright © 2022 by Isabelle Guarino.

All rights reserved. This book or any portion thereof may not be reproduced or used in any manner whatsoever without the express written permission of the publisher except for the use of brief quotations in a book review.

Publishing Services provided by Paper Raven Books LLC

Printed in the United States of America

First Printing, 2022

Paperback ISBN: 978-1-7343153-8-7

Hardback ISBN: 978-1-7343153-9-4

Table of Contents

FILL IT

THE FUTURE

DEDICATION

This book is written for my father, Gene Guarino. He was a wonderful father, a legendary leader, and a spectacular boss. To this day, when someone comes up to share a memory, it's always laced with positivity and reflection on his impact in their life. He touched so many, from those in our trainings, to those he worked with over the years, to neighbors, friends and family. Truly, he was my best friend, my inspiration and the most positive person I have ever known. I am blessed to be able to share this book with the world, and I truly believe it signifies that we caught what he taught.

PART 1

Why Residential Assisted Living?

CHAPTER 1
My Father's Story

In 2012, my dad received a phone call that his mom, my 87-year-old grandmother, had fallen and broken her hip. The doctors said that she would require 24/7 care and would no longer be able to live on her own. Suddenly, my dad and his six siblings were faced with a series of difficult questions about what to do next. Should they provide in-home care, which would be incredibly expensive? If so, who would pay for it? Or should one sibling quit their job to become her full-time caregiver? If so, who would do it? Or… should they put her into a… home?

The idea of sending their beloved mother to a facility made them sick to their stomachs. My grandmother, Marie, had dedicated her career to giving back to others through teaching and education as a nursing professor. A woman of that day and age was not often found in a prestigious profession, but as with everything else in life, she was an exceptional woman. In addition to raising seven children and providing for her family, she was also a caregiver to her own mother and then to her husband, who both fell ill. She was the star of our family and had passed along her inventive, entrepreneurial spirit to all of her children. So, putting her in a "home" after everything she had done for them seemed like a disservice. However, a decision needed to be made. They opted for in-home care as a short-term solution, but at $17,000 a month, it would not be sustainable for very long. Dad vowed to find another option.

He searched all of the assisted living options in upstate New York and was disgusted. Nothing was suitable; everything was so institutional, so impersonal, so… miserable! He flew back to Arizona, his home at the time, and he started searching for options there. Millions of seniors flock to the Southwest during the winter months, so surely there had to be better options than in New York. He toured some facilities but found nothing. Then, one day, he stumbled upon a home, a Residential Assisted Living home in a single-family neighborhood with only 10 residents. They had staff who provided full-time care and who seemed to really love the residents, a unique quality he had not seen in touring any other facilities.

He started speaking with the owner of the home and asked her about the industry. Having been a real estate professional for 40 years, he couldn't help himself. She was kind enough to entertain his questions.

Then he asked, "So, is this one for sale?"

She grabbed him by the arm and swept him into the small office down the hall. "Actually, I have to claim bankruptcy, and selling this house would help me. Would you be open to purchasing it?"

My dad was intrigued by the offer, so he replied, "Show me the numbers and let's talk!"

My father was excited to finally find a place that he and his siblings could afford and feel confident that their mother was receiving the best care. Discovering that there was an investment opportunity was an added bonus. Over the next few months, they worked together on the sale of the business. The owner was an immigrant from Romania who had learned the ins and outs of the business on her own; in exchange for passing along her knowledge to my dad, he helped her work through the bankruptcy.

Before the sale was complete, my grandmother passed. Fortunately, he and his siblings had been able to provide in-home care, in addition to having my two aunts help, to keep her comfortable throughout her final days. Knowing how impossibly expensive that was and knowing that many of the larger, more affordable facilities were lacking in quality of care, my father saw his recent investment as potentially having a real positive impact on the other families who found themselves in similar predicaments. With the coming "silver tsunami" due to an aging population, there would definitely be an increased need for affordable, quality homes to care for elderly loved ones.

Once he started down this investment road, he could not stop. He sold all the other properties he owned. When others asked him what he was doing these days, he said, "I'm doing one thing and one thing only: Residential Assisted Living!" Many of his friends and real estate colleagues had not even heard of it. They started asking my father to show them the properties and tell them more. He was protective of the seniors in his home, though; they had become like family to him. He was reluctant to let the real estate investors into the world of Residential Assisted Living and worried that greedy investors would take over. He wanted to ensure that seniors were being properly cared for. My dad was only 53 years old, and he had already lost both his parents; he understood what it was like to care for aging parents in their final days. He loved his newfound industry, and he loved the impact he was making on both the seniors and their families. So, he was cautious about who he let into his world, wanting to make sure they had the right heart and cared about the people, not just the money.

His long-time friend, Steve, a prominent real estate investor, showed intense interest in learning more. He said, "Gene, tell me what you're doing. I can tell it's something big. I've never seen you so fulfilled and excited about one project. I have to know!" When my dad told him that he had sold all of his other properties to focus on Residential Assisted Living, Steve was confused. He had not been in the loop about my grandmother's needs and how this industry had totally captured my father's heart.

So, my dad divulged, "Well, my mother, Marie, needed care and a home. I realized the best place for her was in a house, a residential house, not a big building like we always think is the only solution. So, I hunted for a place like that back home in New York and found nada! Then I discovered Residential Assisted Living. Seeing the return on investment, the market trends, and the major supply shortage and understanding its impact on families, my heart and wallet both found peace with this new venture.

This is a problem for many families with elderly loved ones, and I knew I could make a major difference."

Steve was stunned and wanted to learn everything my dad knew. This conversation and the many that followed prompted my dad to combine his newfound love for Residential Assisted Living with his lifelong passion for teaching. He was a legend in the real estate training industry; many professionals trusted his advice and wanted to follow what he did. He was always honest and truthful in his interactions, and his heart shone through all of his books, podcasts, infomercials, webinars, and live events.

He decided to create a mini course on Residential Assisted Living. His first class had 13 students. He rented a big bus and drove them around Phoenix to view his properties. He was a one-man show! Like everything he did in life, he gave it all he had. At the end of the three days, his students said, "Okay, so now what?! Who do we call when we need help? Can we call you?" My dad had given them everything he had to offer, so this was a component of mentorship that hadn't crossed his mind. But he never passed up an opportunity.

"Yes," he replied. "Give me a call if you need anything." When they called, he would take notes on areas where they were seeking advice as a way to better prepare for the next class. With his second group of students, he created documents and tutorial videos, which became a package he offered to real estate professionals in the area.

There were so many others in the world just like him who needed to care for an aging loved one, who were not comfortable with the status quo offerings, who wanted to be proud of the options they presented to their parents and loved ones, and who didn't have endless capital. He also saw the financial side from an investment standpoint, which was very profitable; his first three Residential Assisted Living homes each earned between $10,000 to $15,000 per month each. It was a win-win situation.

***

My dad's big heart earned trust from everyone he met. Many people were drawn to his positive energy. It's an indescribable thing to speak and have people know that you are being genuine and truthful and to honor everyone you come in contact with. My dad was a star at that. He let his heart shine first and his words come second. People saw that and gravitated towards it. He was the kind of guy who collected friends and colleagues who wanted to stay in touch with him over the years. He had friends from when he was 14 years old and friends from his latest event. He wasn't overly friendly; he was just… open. He had that "I'm all ears" understanding energy, and that was magnetic. After all, everyone just wants to be seen and heard. The real estate investor industry can be harsh. Some people are sharks, and others just aren't that willing to share what they know, but he was different. That is why he was so beloved.

In October 2021, my dad was teaching a training and did an exercise that he would often do with his classes called "Someday." It was about living every moment to the fullest. He showed 100 small boxes on the screen and said, "You know, statistically we're not going to live to 100," and he crossed out the last 15 boxes at the bottom. Then he said, "And we weren't born yesterday," and started crossing out the boxes at the top. Along the way, he marked special years with a heart: the year he married my mom, the years each of his kids was born, the years each of his three grandkids was born. When he landed on the 60th box, which represented how old he was, he said, "I don't know how many full moons I have left; I hope many more, but if God takes me tomorrow, I know I did what I was supposed to do. I know I came here and learned and listened and grew and taught. I know I served my purpose for the Lord." Little did he know, that would be the last box he would ever check off. The following week, he fell ill, went to the hospital a few days later, and within three weeks, he was gone. His someday had come.

I thank God every day that my dad had an incredible 60 years and that I had 30 years with him. He was the best father in the world. He led by example, he cared, he showed up, and he invested in each of us and our lives. He meant so much to so many people. At his celebration of life ceremony, there were more than 200 family members, friends, and loved ones in attendance and another 2,000 people who showed their support by watching online. Gene Guarino was a mover and a shaker, he was a world-changer, but to me, he was and always will be Dad.

CHAPTER 2
Continuing My Father's Legacy

Gene Guarino started his Residential Assisted Living business as a solo-preneur, but over time, he needed more help. I was working as a flight attendant at the time and noticed my dad was in major need of an assistant. I found myself wandering into his office to help on all of my off days. After a while, I approached him about joining his company and being a part of his vision. Soon after, I quit my job and started working with him full-time. I had fallen in love with the industry and working side-by-side with him. He consistently gave me more and more responsibility and opportunities to learn and grow, and we formed a very solid working relationship.

I felt so good about the work I was doing. We started slowly hiring more people to take on various roles, and we kept one another's visions and dreams close to our day-to-day work and mission. I was the only one of all my siblings to be working with my dad at this point. This wasn't a business we grew up thinking we were going to take over someday, but eventually, we were all drawn to it for different reasons and in different ways.

In 2017, my dad invited my brother, Emmanuel, to go on a cruise, where he had the unique experience of meeting a slew of legends in the real estate industry, including Tom Hopkins, Russel Gray, and Robert Kiyosaki. My brother spent one-on-one time with each of these incredible men, and they all shared insight on taking life to the next level. After the cruise, Emmanuel knew he wanted to start working with my dad. So, he earned his real estate license and asked my father how he could help. My dad showed him what we would need, and my brother started his own side business becoming one of the top realtors in Arizona for buying and selling assisted living homes. It was amazing to see him grab onto something, go for it, and work so hard to become the best of the best.

Three years later, our team had grown from just the two of us to almost 40 people. Instead of relying on me to do all of our marketing, we now had a full-blown marketing machine of a tcam. We had built an incredible company, selling over $15 million in product and attending hundreds of events. I had booked my dad on TV programs, podcasts, and radio shows. We had travelled the world together to promote him and the company. I had found my calling in working with my dad to build businesses and to bring his dreams to reality! I loved learning with him, growing with him, spending time with him, and getting to know him as a talented professional.

One day, we were in an all-team meeting when we decided that it was time to find a second speaker to share our message. We were booking too many events, and there was only one Gene. But who else could step up and represent us? Everyone looked around the room at each other, considering if anyone at the table would be a good fit. My dad knew plenty of people he could call on to come speak, but he wanted something different. He pulled me aside and said, "Isabelle, how about you? Would you like to speak at these events and represent the company out on the road?"

"NO, DAD! No way!" I said shyly but with great conviction. Truly in my heart, I knew I could do it, but I was afraid. He accepted my answer with a smile and a quick look of disappointment. When we went back into the room, I locked eyes with Emmanuel, and I could see he wanted the spot. I pointed at Emmanuel and said loudly, "It's the year of Emmanuel rising!"

For the next four years, I booked my brother on over 50 podcasts, a TEDx stage, and hundreds of speaking sessions. We took every opportunity that came our way. The plan was for Emmanuel to take over the on-stage presence portion of the business for my father when he retired. We had promoted him and had built business relationships with the understanding that he was next in line. After our dad passed, I watched him sacrifice so much the week before his first 3-Day Fast Track event. He was completely devoted to making the presentation his own and somehow managed to do all of this while processing his grief and pain. My brother rocked it for the next four events, but with the loss of our dad and the birth of his newborn son, he was taking on too much. After many long and hard conversations, we all decided that it was not the right timing for him. We started hunting for a new speaker, perhaps one of our past students-turned-success-story. In one of our all-team meetings, our business coach dismissed everyone from the room except for me.

"Isabelle, why not you? Why are you not stepping up?" He stared me dead in the eyes. I burst into tears. Since my dad had passed, I had been given signs that he was still with me. I saw butterflies and heard wind chimes everywhere, and even his favorite song "Celebration" seemed to be playing all the time. He was with me; I knew it. And I knew what he wanted me to do. When I was young, he would follow me with a camera and film "episodes" of my life. He saw something in me that I couldn't see in myself. He knew that my heart was genuine, that I was his legacy.

Our business coach called me on the carpet. He knew my dad's wishes. I cried and cried and didn't know what to say. Then I heard the words come out of my mouth: "Okay, I'll do it." For the first time ever, I chose me. I chose what I needed and wanted in that moment: authenticity to my truest self.

Over the course of the next six weeks, we "built my celebrity," which was HARD and uncomfortable! I had spent the last eight years completely out of the spotlight. I had hidden myself because I did not want the attention on me. Everyone in the industry knew me, but no one on the outside knew me. I took to TikTok, www.tiktok.com/@ral.academy, to start making silly videos to showcase myself and the brand. I booked myself on podcasts, radio shows, webinars, and stages. My first in-person live event was a 60-minute time slot on Think Realty's stage in Houston. I had done many virtual events over the previous weeks, but this was my first time presenting in front of a live audience. I was excited and nervous.

I had practiced my speech at home so many times that both of my dogs knew how to open assisted living homes!

The night before my speech, I could barely sleep. I kept seeing a message in my mind that said "You got this." My dad was sending me his encouragement. I knew he was proud. He was never overwhelming with encouragement but was encouraging enough to show that he really, genuinely believed in you. If my dad believed in me, then I could believe in myself too. The next morning, I took the stage. I had the time of my life sharing my heart of the assisted-living industry and my journey up to that point. When my presentation was over, I was bum-rushed by a dozen people who wanted to share their stories with me, to connect. I understood how they felt and their struggles. It was a beautiful full-circle moment. I realized this was exactly where I needed to be.

3-DAY FAST TRACK EVENT

One week later, it was time for me to take the stage at our 3-Day Fast Track event where students learn how to own and operate their own Residential Assisted Living care homes. We teach the national standards on how to start your home using four methods, how to fund your home using seven different funding sources, and how to not just survive but thrive in this business by doing good and doing well. We teach our students to fill their homes with the proper staffing and residents for long-term success in their new venture.

Speaking from a stage is one thing, but selling is something else. I had watched my father do this for many years but had never done anything like this myself. My brother had four years of speaker training under his belt. When he performed, he was seamless. He knew where to stand, how to pause, and what to look for in the audience. I was going in blind. With adrenaline coursing through my body, I walked to the conference room, took a few deep breaths, and walked up on stage. The thrilling experience of sharing my heart was absolutely what I needed to prove that I had it inside me to continue this legacy.

You see, my father left me with the most incredible blessing: three cash-flowing Residential Assisted Living homes. I felt a calling, a burning desire, a true passion to share with others the three solutions that one assisted living residence offers:

1. a home for a loved one when they need it,

2. a home for yourself so you don't have to worry about what happens to you when you need assisted living care, and

3. a blessing to pass to your heirs or children so they can be financially secure and help other families.

We are on the brink of this industry really taking off, so there is no better time to get involved than now. There are 77 million baby boomers, with 10,000 people turning 65 and 4,000 people turning 85 each day in the United States, and those numbers continue to rise. At the peak, it is expected that 11,500 people will be turning 85 every single day! They will need options for care, and they deserve more than just a big-box facility.

At the end of the first day following a jam-packed session of education and bus tours of the Residential Assisted Living homes, I was excited to share more. The many one-on-one conversations with my students throughout the day had revealed that people were deeply interested in the opportunity to work with our team. All of my fears melted away because I realized I was providing them exactly what they wanted. At the end of the session, I announced, "Class is officially over, but if you want to stick around for 10 minutes to learn how you could work with our team, I'd love to show you how! There's no pressure. You're welcome to go. We will see you at 9 a.m. tomorrow. Thank you!" Just as my father used to say. I turned around to drink a sip of water, expecting to have a lull as people left, when all of a sudden the room broke out with cheering. Everyone was still in their seats, and their eyes were locked on me. They were ready for more! I delivered my pitch on the products and services we had to offer, and I watched as their hearts opened to the opportunity to learn more and to grow with us.

Being open and honest with an audience about an industry that means so much to my family, that changed our lives and gave us a chance to do good and do well, was the most incredible feeling. I knew in that moment that Dad was proud. My number one priority was and always will be pouring all my knowledge and insight into our students, making sure they have all the tools they need to succeed once they leave our training.

That night, 35 students committed to moving forward with their business. For me, though, it wasn't about the number of people choosing to work with us on an ongoing basis. More importantly, it was about the right people choosing to begin this type of work. I prayed long and hard prior to the event that the right people would show up, that the wrong people would have their hearts harden, that it would be abundantly clear who was or wasn't good for our team. On that first day of the event, it was evident that my prayers had been heard.

This type of investment is not just about money; it's also about touching others' lives and leaving a positive impact on the world. So on the final day of the event, I shared with my students how Residential Assisted Living provides not only a pathway to financial success but also opens up opportunities to give back to others. I described a trip to Jamaica that was a pivotal moment in determining my future.

When I was still working as a flight attendant and was deciding whether I wanted to continue with that career or join my dad in his assisted living ventures, I went on a mission trip with a group of friends to visit and work in a church, teaching a summer Bible school.

The church leaders arranged a visit to a home for seniors on the final day of our trip. When we arrived at Denham Town Golden Age Retirement home, my heart broke. The smell, the amenities, the food, the building was absolutely terrible! It was like walking into the "thrown-away members of society" home. Their diet was limited to rice, beans, bananas, ackee, and mangos, they didn't have vitamins or medications, and there were no books, or games. They sat around all day and talked; they seemed to spend most of their time crying. I knew God placed me there for a reason and that I had to do something.

Upon returning home, I met with my dad and told him I wanted to come work for him but that I wanted to do something for this community in Jamaica. He loved the idea, so I went to work! Three years later, we hosted our first Residential Assisted Living National Convention (www.ralnatcon.com). It was the perfect time to raise money to go back to Denham Town and bless this senior home. With the $15,000 that people donated, we were able to return to Denham to purchase all of the supplies the home needed, including diapers, clothes, shoes, medicine, and games. We went with the staff to the grocery store to buy $3,000 worth of food and filled eight shopping carts with everything from juice, oatmeal, and frozen meats and vegetables to candies, ice cream, and cake since the seniors had not had dessert in years. Finally, after learning that the manager of the property, Calvin, only made $2,000 each year, we wrote him a check for $5,000. He cried so hard that we didn't even know what to do.

We were so happy to be there to help them in any way we could, and this experience filled my heart with indescribable joy. Whether it's in business or in life, with money or with time and energy, giving to others is what makes the world go round. As I told this story on stage, I could see that our students resonated with the sentiment. They loved the idea of giving back, and I was invigorated to share that part of my heart with them, connecting and growing together as a community at an even deeper level. When you see the smile and relief that money can do for someone in need, that feeling never goes away.

Since then, I have been graciously able to be a guest on over 50+ podcasts, I have spoken to 1000s of investors live and in person, as well as, entrepreneurs and medical professionals on the topic of Residential Assisted Living. I was named "Top Influencer in Senior Housing." I have been able to host multiple 3-Day training events and our annual RAL National Convention twice. Connect with students across the country and help aid them in opening their own RAL homes. It has been truly life changing for me. When fear becomes obsolete and everything aligns the world feels pretty good. It's never the wrong time to do the right thing and I knew in my heart this was my chance, my calling. I'm so glad I listened to all the signs, to all the buildup, to my own internal peace. I am blessed to lead RAL Academy. I am blessed to teach from the same stage as my father. I am lucky to be able to carry his legacy forward in such an honest, true and intentional manner. His shoes are big, but I'm up for the challenge.

CHAPTER 3

Why Invest in Residential Assisted Living

There are many reasons why Residential Assisted Living (RAL) is an attractive investment. Most importantly, it provides a solution to the caregiver crisis, and it improves the lives of seniors and the adult children of aging parents. Big-box facilities are just not home. They aren't a single-family setting, they don't have a regular kitchen table, they don't smell good, and they are just not pleasant places to be in general.

One of our incredible students experienced firsthand this heartbreaking reality. His grandmother lived in one of these facilities, and when he went to visit her one day, he discovered that the monthly bill for her stay had doubled. He asked the staff why the charges had increased. The staff replied that his grandmother was refusing to take showers and was fighting the staff, so it required two staff members and more time, which increased the cost.

At first, he was understanding of why that would be the case. But when he asked his grandmother about it, she told a different story. She said that a woman would come into her room and would just start ripping off her clothes and pushing her into the bathroom. His grandmother felt violated, so she would fight the person off. Then the next day, they would bring in two people she had never seen, and they would pin her down and do the same thing. He was mortified! He understood the facility was having issues working with his grandmother, but he also understood why his grandmother was terrified and fighting them. On top of that, she was starting to have memory issues, and with so many staff members coming and going, the lack of personal connection was making everything worse.

He knew his grandmother wasn't receiving the care she deserved and needed in that facility. Unfortunately, in many of these larger facilities, they actually tell the care staff to not personally connect with the residents. They think that if they treat the residents like numbers and don't connect with them, the staff will be able to tolerate staying there for longer because they avoid being distressed when residents pass away. This sad, misguided approach leads to inhumane and even abusive living conditions that are destructive for both the residents and the staff.

By investing in RAL, we can provide an incredible opportunity to the caregivers and medical professionals in this industry. People are usually drawn to the medical field because they want to care for others and make a difference. Then they get thrown into an environment that does the exact opposite. They are often disappointed by the low level of care they are physically able to provide because they are so overworked. There is just no way they can be there for everyone in the way that they need. But when you give those caregivers, nurses, and administrators a chance in an RAL home, they thrive!

Over the years, I have had many conversations with caregivers from these big facilities. Often, they break down and cry as they share how they have to care for 50 residents every day with very little support from the top. The families are demanding, their schedules are wild, and they are simply burnt out. When we ask them if they would be open to coming to work at our homes and tell them about the five-to-one resident to caregiver ratio, the upscale single-family home, and the location in a nearby neighborhood, they jump at the chance. You can make a huge difference in the caregivers' lives by creating the opportunity to let them truly use their hearts in their work. We have seen so many professional caregivers go from broken to fulfilled in a matter of weeks!

Of course, RAL investments also provide good homes for the seniors. Currently in assisted living are the 41 million seniors known as "The Silent Generation." Many of them require long-term assisted living care, in an already limited amount of space. Soon, we will have 76 million baby boomers reaching the age where they need care. How in the world are we going to have good options for 76 million seniors, when we are already facing a crisis of limited care, lack of beds, and inhumane living conditions for the current 41 Million? This is why I am so passionate about helping investors and entrepreneurs start their own RAL homes! These seniors will need someplace to go, and I can't do it alone. Our students can create gorgeous homes for them and can help solve this massive crisis our country is facing. Currently, 61 percent of all assisted living beds are in assisted living homes with fewer than 25 beds. This means that, more often than not, seniors actually end up in smaller care homes. We are not a niche market; we are just the quiet ones flying under the radar because our marketing dollars aren't as strong. As soon as someone hears about this concept, they are so excited to visit our homes and to learn that there are other options.

Finally, we can't forget about the adult children in these scenarios. When Daughter Judy (as we affectionately call the adult child of an aging parent) starts looking for a place for her mom, she is feeling all sorts of emotions: guilty, angry, scared, nervous, overwhelmed. My dad and his siblings felt the same when they were searching for a place for my grandmother. Many adult children really struggle during this transitional time because so much comes with the process. It's not just finding a place that suits Mom or Dad; it's cleaning out and selling their home, dealing with all their belongings, figuring out the finances, negotiating roles with family members, and preparing for situations they have never had to deal with before. Who is going to visit when, and what does this time commitment look like for you now? What if you have a resistant parent who is upset and refuses to leave their home? What if your siblings halfway across the country are trying to give their input? What if your mom or dad has memory care issues and can't even remember who they are? What if your partner isn't supportive? What if you have young children and are now having to divide your time and attention to care for your parent?

Adult children who are charged with finding care for an aging parent take on a huge strain, both emotionally and financially. A little empathy for Daughter Judy goes a long way. Teaching students who are in these scenarios is my life's greatest blessing. I love to give them that moment of relief, that deep breath, when they understand that owning and operating an RAL can relieve this burden of stress not only for other seniors and families but also their own parents and loved ones. It gives me such peace knowing that I can help them answer tough questions, breathe more easily, and move forward in a positive, progressive way. As famed American salesman and motivational speaker Zig Ziglar once said, "You will get all you want in life, if you help enough other people get what they want."

Owning an RAL home also creates a cash flow for you. Let's compare the RAL option with three primary alternatives to earning income when you own a single-family home: flipping, renting to tenants, and vacation-home hosting. Many people get their start in real estate by purchasing a home in need of updates and repairs, fixing it up to add value, and selling or flipping it to make a lump sum of money. This can be a great option, but it does not earn you a steady cash flow; with every home you purchase, you are essentially buying yourself another job. It's cash NOW, not cash flow. A second option would be to rent out your home to a family or a group of students. Many investors who focus on single family investing say this is more drama than it's worth. Even if you are fortunate enough to earn $1,000 a month on one of these properties, there could be punches in the wall, the destroyed bathrooms, the motorcycles in the living rooms, the broken windows, the parties…. nope, no, no thank you! Finally, there are vacation rental services like Airbnb. Although I love the concept of Airbnb and it is such a fun investment play, it won't create consistent cash flow during difficult times. When inflation is going crazy, a recession hits, or times get tough, people stop spending money on vacations.

RAL is not a luxury expense; it's a necessity. Mom or Dad's care and housing is not optional. It's not something you just cut out or stop paying. You make it happen. And the statistics show us that there is a demand for beds for seniors. As of 2021, there were only 996,100 beds that currently existed in the assisted living market, yet there were 3,880,240 seniors who might need assistance. The need far outweighs the supply we currently have, and we can't build RAL homes fast enough.

Senior housing is the best play in real estate and business and will be the best play for at least the next few decades. Cash flow and demand is found in one market and one market only: assisted living. There is less drama than single-family rentals, it's not dependent on a strong market like Airbnb, and it offers cash flow, unlike flipping homes. It's steady, it's needed, and it's proven.

But money is only part of the equation. What about helping others? How many real estate investors in these other sectors receive love letters, flowers, balloons, hugs, and heartfelt text messages and phone calls monthly from multiple families? Probably none. As owners of RAL homes, we receive that love and recognition ALL THE TIME because the families are so grateful. They are overjoyed to have their loved one in a home with owners who care, who make an effort, who treat their family member with decency and respect. The work that we are doing in this sector is impactful and important. Investing in this category pays out in dividends you would never expect.

One of our incredible students, Monique, said, "I never expected how much opening my RAL home would open my heart too. I now have 10 grandmas, and even though I don't have to, I love to visit my home and hang out with them, hear their stories, and connect with them. It makes my world go round to be able to bless them in their last years of life. I feel blessed that I stumbled into my calling to serve others with RAL after attending your course."

Two of our other students, Alyssa and Zach, opened their care home in New York, where they provide care to Alyssa's grandmother. She shared with us, "I have been able to spend more quality time with my grandma than I ever have before. I know she's getting top-notch quality care and love, and my entire family is so thankful for me opening my RAL home. Not only am I cash-flowing, but I'm also providing solutions, and I've built such a strong and beautiful relationship with my beloved grandma. I am forever thankful for this opportunity opening my eyes to this type of investing."

CHAPTER 4

Is Owning a Residential Assisted Living Facility for You?

In Part 2, we will be diving into all the details of how to get started with owning a Residential Assisted Living (RAL) facility and how to set yourself up for success. But first, let's look at what it takes to do this work and explore whether this is right for *you*.

Over the years, we have seen that students who are successful in owning an RAL facility have three qualities in common:

1. They have a passion for helping people and care about seniors.

2. They have a strong WHY.

3. They have grit.

The truth is that not everyone can or should do this work. While this is a highly rewarding endeavor, there are also many barriers to entry. There's a reason that HGTV doesn't have any shows about this (although they've asked us to try). It's just not all that simple. It takes someone who is willing to jump through hoops and who is willing to get knocked down, get back up, and keep trying. I would much rather have you figure out now that this is not the right path for you rather than investing in a home, renovating it, moving seniors in, hiring your staff, and then realizing that you're in the wrong industry.

CARING FOR OTHERS

First, RAL owners need to have genuine care and concern for seniors. And what we're really talking about is a passion for helping people in general because there are a lot of different people involved with assisted living. Do you care about others? Are you a kind and thoughtful person who is willing to communicate from the heart with adult children, caregivers, and other industry professionals? If you cannot get into that heart space, this is going to be hard for you. Remember Daughter Judy? It's an incredibly difficult time in her life. She lost her mom as she once knew her. She is feeling angry, sad, mad, guilty, hurt, lost, alone, depressed, overwhelmed, and maybe even relieved, hopeful, and thankful. Can you meet her where she's at and reach into the heart of the conversation? If so, you're going to be just fine!

It's a hard time for the senior, too. Do you want someone to come into your home and tell you that you can no longer live alone and must have a babysitter 24/7? Do you want someone telling you that you aren't capable? That you're not safe? That they're scared for you? And how does it feel that your own children are telling you this? Many seniors have a lot of pride and may also be lonely and depressed. They are frustrated. Many of their friends are passing on, and maybe even their partner has passed. They're just trying to make it day by day. Maybe they're losing their memory, or their body no longer functions as well. The experience may look and feel very different for a senior who is losing their memory than a senior who loses their body functionality and still has a sharp mind. But no matter what happens, aging isn't always fun.

YOUR WHY

Having a strong WHY is a major point of paralysis for some people. You have to dig to the root of the WHY. For example, you want to buy some new cologne. Why do you do that? You don't just buy a new cologne to buy a new cologne. You buy the cologne to smell good. WHY? You want to smell good for someone because you want to attract them.

WHY? You want to attract them because you want a partner. WHY? You want a partner because you want kids. WHY? You want kids to feel more fulfilled and to live out your life's dream. So truly you bought the cologne because you want to feel fulfilled. This is how deep I need you to get with your WHY!

Take out a piece of paper and write down your top five reasons why you want to open a Residential Assisted Living home. Then, go through each of those reasons and ask yourself WHY five times, digging more deeply with each answer. You may land on the same deep-rooted reason each time, or each reason may be unique. For me, this exercise looks a little something like this:

Why do I want to open and continue owning an RAL?

Reason 1: Because it helps seniors
WHY? They need quality housing, and it's important that I can provide it.

WHY? Because how can I sit by and watch what's happening and not do something when I know what needs to be done?

WHY? Because I have the power of capital, resources, and knowledge.

WHY? Because I was blessed so I could bless others.

WHY? Because it makes me feel like a better person; I feel proud of myself when I can give back and help others in an impactful and contributing manner.

My true WHY is I have self-pride and feel good when I give back.

Reason 2: Because it brings in great cash flow
WHY? $10,000 a month on one of these homes is incredible, and I love to have that cash flow for my family.

WHY? Because I want to live a certain lifestyle.

WHY? Because I want my spouse and future kids to have everything they need.

WHY? Because I want to provide the best of the best for them; I want them to feel and be secure financially.

WHY? Because I know what it feels like to struggle, and it scares me that my kids may have to understand that. I want to protect them and give them everything in my power to provide the best life for them possible.

My true WHY is I want to provide my family with financial security.

Reason 3: Because it provides better jobs for caregivers

WHY? They go into this industry to help people, and then they get overworked and underpaid; that makes me feel bad.

WHY? I feel bad because they are really trying; they have big hearts, but they're not being given the opportunity to shine for the seniors.

WHY? Because the system is broken, and if I can do something to improve it, I want to.

WHY? Because I am in a place of power, and it's my job to do what I can to support our community, provide jobs, and be an incredible boss.

WHY? Because I was blessed to bless others, and if I don't give them what they need, who will? It is my burden to carry.

My true WHY is I have a responsibility to do this work.

Reason 4: Because it's needed

WHY? Because the baby boomers are aging into a stage of life where they will need more care.

WHY? There are physically not enough beds, and there is no true plan for where they will all live and how they will be cared for.

WHY? Because we rely on government too much and no one is coming together to provide a solution.

WHY? Because people don't care about things until they happen to them. It's time to care for things we may not see yet, for things that may not affect us personally. It's time to care.

WHY? Because if we don't, we will have a massive crisis, and I don't want to know I could have done something and instead just sat on my hands. It's important for me to take action with the knowledge I have.

My true WHY is taking action feels good to me, and ignorance doesn't.

Reason 5: Because it's a legacy play

WHY? My dad passed this huge blessing to me, and I want to pass it to my future kids.

WHY? Because having cash in the bank or a trust is cool, but passing on a legacy business would be even cooler.

WHY? Because it means something; it has value and purpose, and how cool would it be that it will have been owned by three generations of Guarinos?!

WHY? Because I believe my dad would be proud of me.

WHY? Because I know he worked hard to create these businesses; I can tell my kids the stories about my dad and me working together, and it will come full circle and fill my heart with joy.

My true WHY is I want to make my father proud.

At the end of the day, my WHYs started as the following: helping seniors; great cash flow; providing better jobs for the caregivers; it's needed; and it's a legacy play. In doing this exercise, I discovered that my true WHYs are actually the following:

- I have self-pride and feel good when I give back.
- I want to provide my family with financial security.
- I have a responsibility to do this work.
- Taking action feels good to me and ignorance doesn't.
- I want to make my father proud.

GRIT

The word "grit" can mean so many things depending on who you ask. According to Angela Duckworth, PhD, a psychologist who has studied and written extensively about this topic, grit is defined as "perseverance and passion for long-term goals."

To break it down into an acronym, grit means,
>   **G**uts

>   **R**esilience

>   **I**nitiative

>   **T**enacity

And it can also mean…

Give it your all

Redo if necessary

Ignore giving up

Take time to do it right

From my perspective, grit is the ability to have the courage and bravery to do things that others may deem impossible. To overcome obstacles no matter how big they may seem. To have that in-depth, innate, soul-harnessing power to choose this over anything. To be relentless in your pursuit. To never give up, never cave in, and never stop until you achieve success. This industry can be tough. It can break you. When you get no after no, when people around you tell you to just give up… it's going to be hard to stick to your guns. But with grit on your side, you can and will do it.

Outwitting the Devil by Napoleon Hill tells the story of a gentleman who has a conversation with the devil. When the devil proclaims that he controls 98 percent of the population, the man asks him how he does it. The devil shares with him that all he has to do is convince people to drift. If they drift, they aren't committing, they aren't dedicated, and they aren't on fire, so they give up easily. They will live a life of apathy, indifference, and laziness. When your grit starts to wane—and inevitably it will—remember this and say, "No way am I going to let the devil win today! No freaking way!" And push harder than you ever have before.

Whether or not you are religious, we can all relate to this sentiment. There will always be those who try to dim your flame. Keep your strong heart for seniors, stay focused on your whys, and hold on to your grit for dear life, and nothing can stand in your way. Owning a Residential Assisted Living home isn't easy, but when you know why you're doing it and keep your eyes on the bigger picture, the rewards always outweigh the sacrifices, the fear, the risk. When you persevere through the difficult times, you will succeed.

CHAPTER 5

Debunking the Eight Myths of Residential Assisted Living

You probably have a lot of questions about owning a Residential Assisted Living (RAL) facility, and you might have some concerns about investing in this industry. So, let's talk about the top eight myths of RAL.

Myth #1: You to have to work in the home.

Myth #2: You need to be a medical professional.

Myth #3: The liability will be through the roof.

Myth #4: COVID-19 has killed all the seniors.

Myth #5: There are no seniors in your area, since they all moved to Florida or Arizona.

Myth #6: Your neighborhood/city/county/state will never allow this.

Myth #7: Seniors cannot afford this.

Myth #8: It's impossible to find and keep excellent employees.

MYTH #1:

YOU HAVE TO WORK IN THE HOME

To start, you do not have to do anything you don't want to do. I was not born to be a caregiver, and you may not have been either, and that is perfectly fine! You can play whatever role you like as the owner of the real estate or the business. This is your business, and if you set it up the way we have done and we suggest you do, you will be able to work ON the business, not IN it. That is always my personal goal for each of our students in the 3-Day Fast Track classes. I want to help you discover your individual goals and then help you accomplish them. So, if working in the home is not part of your vision, then don't allow it. Set yourself up to hire the proper team so you can be hands-off. Building that team with the right people in the right seats is vital, and it's the first step to solidifying your own role within the business.

MYTH #2:

YOU NEED TO BE A MEDICAL PROFESSIONAL

Although licensing is necessary on several levels in RAL facilities, you do not need to be a medical professional to get into this industry. The physical home will have a license, which is primarily relevant to the flow, layout, and safety within the home for the seniors. The administrator will be licensed through your state, and they will be running the day-to-day operations for you. The caregivers will also likely be licensed through your state, as they will be responsible for the care of the residents, the cleanliness of the home, the cooking, etc. You are not working in the home, so you do not need to be licensed. Think about it like this: does the person who owns the McDonald's building need to know how to work the cash register or flip the burgers? No! Does that person get called when someone doesn't show up to their shift? No! The manager takes care of the daily operations, including training, hiring, firing, and fixing staffing issues. The owner of the real estate is not involved in the day-to-day drama or issues. It's similar in a care home. You, the owner of the real estate and the business, are not responsible for the care of the residents. Since you are not responsible for what medications they are taking or what food they are eating, you do not need any kind of medical licensing.

MYTH #3:

THE LIABILITY WILL BE THROUGH THE ROOF

People often worry about liability in a residential home with seniors. The good news is that insurance on these properties is about $1 to $2 per day per resident, so with 10 residents and 30 days on average in a month, the total per month is typically between $300 to $600. It's truly a line item and not a big issue. In our 3-Day Fast Track training class, we cover this topic in-depth and provide access to resources with insurance agencies that work with us and many of our students; they are able to explain and share with you how to protect and cover yourself.

Now this is not legal advice, as I am not a lawyer and do not claim to be, but I want to share my personal experiences with you. In the eight years we have been in business and with the thousands of students we have trained, I am not aware of anyone having ever been sued for anything that has happened within their homes. Now, I'm not saying it doesn't happen; it definitely can happen. But the biggest key is setting yourself up for success. Make sure to add those ramps and guard rails to reduce fall risk. Keep the home clean and safe at all times. Fix problems as soon as they arise. Set up cameras around the outside of the home and in the shared living spaces so you can keep your eyes on what is happening. Put in place strict policies and procedures and hire an administrator who understands and implements them impeccably. The entire team needs to be on the same page; being slow to hire and quick to fire if anything is ever in question is one of the best pieces of advice I can give!

The goal of insurance and protection is to make sure that your residents are safe and comfortable, their families trust you, and you and your staff are protected in the event that something goes wrong. Letting the small things slip is the fastest way to go downhill, and staying on top of things right when they happen is majorly important in this industry.

MYTH #4:

COVID-19 KILLED ALL THE SENIORS

I know how ridiculous that sounds, but unfortunately, I've heard that claim many times over the course of the last several years. People are often not completely understanding of what actually happened in many assisted living homes versus facilities when COVID-19 hit. The larger facilities had a rude awakening because many people did get sick and died from the disease. The question is why were these facilities hit the hardest? Primarily, these seniors were at increased risk because it is significantly harder to control and contain who comes and goes from those facilities. They have janitors, chefs, front desk staff, caregivers, activities contractors, doctors, nurses, etc. In one facility, there may be 40 or more staff members in and out every single day. The residents have different caregivers every day, going from floor to floor and potentially spreading illness from resident to resident. Within our homes, it's significantly easier to control because we have the same staff day in and day out, usually a maximum of 10 total people on a weekly basis working with the same residents. We've been saying "smaller is better" for a long time!

In 2020, Senior Housing News said it too in their article titled, "Smaller Is Better: Covid-19 Primes Senior Living for Rise of Small-House Models" by Tim Regan.[1] People were desperate to get their loved ones out of large facilities and begging us to take them in. The trends are leaning toward

---

1 https://seniorhousingnews.com/2020/06/03/smaller-is-better-covid-19-primes-senior-living-for-rise-small-house-models/

smaller residential homes with fewer seniors because it's safer, more comfortable, closer to home, and cheaper. It's what's best for many seniors, particularly when facing public health threats such as COVID-19.

MYTH #5:

ALL THE OLD PEOPLE MOVED TO FLORIDA OR ARIZONA

Don't all the seniors move to warmer climates when they are ready to retire? No! Just because you turn 85 doesn't mean you automatically move to Florida or Arizona. Most people who are considering retiring somewhere else will move between the ages of 60 and 70, but if you haven't moved or don't want to move, you're not going to pick up and change your whole life at the age of 85. People tend to stay where they grew up and where their friends and family are.

One of our incredible staff members, Kati, wanted to help her grandmother because she needed care. Kati lived in Utah, and her grandmother lived in Iowa, which is where she grew up. She moved her grandmother to a house not far from her own in Salt Lake City so she could keep an eye on her. She visited with her all the time and thought that she would adjust over time. But her grandmother was so unhappy because she missed Iowa. Within two years, she asked Kati to help her move back. Even though she technically had family close by, she would rather be in her comfort zone, which was Iowa. It makes sense. My grandmother feels the same way. She lives in Florida, and even though we want her closer to us, she refuses to move out to Arizona. She has a knitting club and friends, the streets are familiar, she knows the restaurants and the grocery stores, and she knows what to expect with the weather. When the time comes for her to receive more regular care, we will find an assisted living home for her in Florida because we know that will be the best thing for her.

Keep in mind that people are aging everywhere, and there is opportunity around every corner. There may be different rules and regulations in each state, but these homes exist all over the United States, even in other countries! Plus, there can be an advantage to owning an RAL in places others than Florida and Arizona because it's not always best to invest in a saturated market.

MYTH #6:

YOUR NEIGHBORHOOD WILL NEVER ALLOW THIS

Neighbors and Homeowners Associations (HOAs) may have complaints about you opening an RAL home, but the law is on your side! The Federal Fair Housing Act states, "The Fair Housing Act prohibits discrimination in housing because of race, color, national origin, religion, sex, gender identity or sexual orientation, familial status and/or disability." You can use this law to win most arguments against a state, city, county, neighborhood, or HOA. They cannot legally prevent you from opening your home.

However, they may still try, so we created the RAL National Association (RALNA) to help! Sometimes you just need a little muscle behind you to win the legal argument. The Pinkowski Law group is an incredible team of lawyers who work with RALNA to protect our students and any small care homeowners from unfair discrimination. When a city starts to implement a rule or regulation that favors large group homes instead of being inclusive, the lawyers are right there to report on it and fight this injustice. We are thrilled to be able to offer memberships to anyone in the care home industry or looking to get in at www.RALNA.org.

With RALNA on your side, you have the backing and support you need to win those battle. But why fight when you don't have to? If one neighborhood is putting up a huge fight against you and the other one right across the street could not care less, open your home in the friendlier neighborhood. There's no reason to waste your time, energy, and resources fighting when you don't need to.

Our staff members, Janet and Mark, have a gorgeous RAL home in Ohio. When they first got started, they had angry neighbors who didn't want them to open their home. The neighbors said, "No way are we allowing a business into our neighborhood! You will decrease the value of our homes. There will be old people running around in the streets. You will bring lots of traffic, and there will be firetrucks, police cars, and ambulances here all the time. You can't do this here."

Notice how the uninformed mind jumps to many inaccurate conclusions. However, once you can kindly and calmly debunk many of their presumptions, you can and will win them over. Let's address these concerns one at a time.

Concern: No businesses are allowed in our neighborhood!

Answer: If you won't allow my licensed business to operate within this home, then we will have to play fair for all and shut down all business owners and operators in this neighborhood. That would include but not be limited to any accountants, realtors, work-from-home businesses, etc. Are you willing and able to apply that rule to everyone, and how will I know you are upholding that rule to make it fair for everyone? More than likely someone on the HOA board or in the neighborhood falls into this category, and you will shut that opposition down quickly!

One of our students, Dale, faced this issue in Oregon. He had a neighbor who was putting up huge opposition to his home being "a business in a neighborhood." His argument was that neighborhoods are for families only and businesses shouldn't be allowed. It would bring unnecessary traffic to the area and potentially cause more businesses to want to come into their neighborhood. Dale used his RALNA resources, fought the good fight, and won. He went to the next HOA meeting with a beautiful slideshow with stats and graphs on the positive impact an RAL home has on a neighborhood. He noted that there was another home around the corner that was a care home for seniors and that it had brought zero issues to that neighborhood. Many were not even aware the senior care home existed, which proved Dale's point exactly. He also noted how many members of the HOA were running businesses from within their own homes, including the president, who worked from home as an accountant and used his home address as his business address. He asked if the president would also be willing to shut down his business if Dale's home did not get approved. Of course, the president scoffed at him, but his point came across with great vigor. Many other neighbors were also working from home or using their home address as a business address, and this really helped his case. He also reminded everyone of the Federal Fair Housing Act, provided brochures of his soon-to-be home, and invited everyone to a tour and a discount. Dale brought all his cards to the table. The HOA ultimately approved his plans, and his RAL home is successfully operating today!

Concern: Your business will decrease the value of the homes in our neighborhood!

Answer: We have actually done studies on this using some of our students' care homes with RALNA, and we have not observed any decreases in value within the neighborhood in relation to an RAL home opening. In fact, the modifications you are making to the home are usually making the home larger and adding more bedrooms and bathrooms, which makes your physical property even more valuable. In turn, this increases the value of all nearby homes. If you do create this business and then sell the real estate portion of it, you will more than likely be making a profit, so the increase in value you are bringing actually helps the neighborhood from this angle.

Scott and Michelle, two students who became staff members, encountered this issue in Louisiana. They had an angry neighbor who petitioned against them very publicly, claiming that opening an RAL would decrease the values of the other homes in the neighborhood. All Scott and Michelle had to do was stay calm and use their RALNA resources to present the facts at their next town hall meeting. They easily won the battle against the angry neighbor using charts, graphs, and statistics from their local area and others nearby. They showcased their other RAL facilities in the area and showed proof of homes selling for the same or higher value after being next to a care home. They left that town hall meeting with an overwhelming vote in favor of their business continuing to be built!

Concern: Old people will be on the loose!

Answer: This is genuinely a concern for some angry neighbors, and again, we have done studies and surveys with our own students' homes and with RALNA to assess to what extent residents escape their facilities. It has happened less than 1 percent of the time across the board in all 50 states. This is a non-issue. For RAL homes that specialize in memory care, they are required to have specific locks on the doors to prevent residents from leaving without supervision. Even for regularly licensed RAL homes, they are also equipped with special locks to help keep the residents safe. Seniors don't go missing in our homes. They don't go even a couple of minutes without having eyes on them. Overseeing six to 16 residents in a small home is much easier than overseeing 50 residents on a large property.

One of our students, Shondra, encountered this issue in Massachusetts. An angry neighbor put up a huge battle in an HOA meeting and shouted, "But the old people will be running around naked and we might hit them with our cars. It's going to be chaos!" Everyone turned their heads to look at the angry neighbor, and chuckles could be heard around the room. Saying it out loud revealed how ridiculous it was, and it gave everyone a good laugh!

Concern: Your business will bring too much traffic to this neighborhood!

Answer: This is a concern often brought up by neighbors and sometimes also HOA boards or city councils. Our students, Donald and Talinda, in Kansas City, Missouri were asked to provide one parking spot per four residents, even though none of the residents drove. It was a very silly request, but since that is what the city required, they were happy to oblige. Sometimes you have to ask yourself how you can make it work. If adding a large circular drive or some extra spots for parking appeases people, then you can do it!

Sometimes the concern is about the increased presence of police cars, fire trucks, or ambulances. If a senior was living alone in that same home and they fell, what would they do? Call the ambulance. If there are up to 16 seniors living in that home, they are being supervised 24/7 and have safety precautions such as ramps, so the odds of falling are much lower. But it can still happen. We cannot control 100 percent of the day-to-day happenings within the home, and a fall takes just one moment of unsupervised movement. So asking the same question again, if up to 16 seniors are living in the same home and one of them falls, what happens? We call the ambulance. Once you explain this to whoever is asking, it helps put the question into perspective about what we are doing by providing care in an RAL home. Ambulances don't just come for fun; they come because something serious happened and someone needs help. If your neighbors can't understand that, you have bigger fish to fry!

Our students, Mike and Jen, had to provide proof that their RAL home would not cause extra traffic in Michigan. Again, RALNA came in handy, and they used their research and data to prove to their neighbors that this was a non-issue. They went to HOA board meetings and city council meetings and continued to stay calm, serene, and purposeful in their communications about their upcoming home. They had plans to open an eight-bed RAL, and they really wanted to make it happen in that specific neighborhood. Once they finally opened their doors, they hosted an open house for all their neighbors. Seeing the home and understanding what they had created and what they planned to do changed most of the neighbors' minds. It wasn't a hospital in a neighborhood, it wasn't an eyesore, it wasn't everything they feared… It was just a single-family home from the outside and a loving, caring, elderly community on the inside. A few of their neighbors actually moved their own parents into the home just a couple of weeks later so they could come by any time to visit since it was in their neighborhood. What a beautiful story of how persistence can pay off!

When you're dealing with someone who has not-in-my-backyard (NIMBY) syndrome, make sure to work with RALNA (www.ralna.org) and be open to conversations where you may have to be persuasive. The key is to make a good impression, let the community know what you're doing, and involve them as much as possible.

MYTH #7:

SENIORS CAN'T AFFORD ASSISTED LIVING

When we talk about the cost of care for assisted living, people can really get their panties in a bunch! I've heard people say over and over again that seniors can't afford this, but that's just not true. First, many seniors can afford it. Not all of them, of course, but many of them. The baby boomer generation holds most of the wealth in our country. Many of them set themselves up with IRAs, savings, and homes that have risen in value. There are many ways people plan to pay for their care needs. So, let's go through them.

Some seniors do have their own money. They have cash in the bank, they have equity, or they plan to use their pension money or an IRA. Some plan to sell their house and use that money for their care needs. About 10 percent of seniors in the US have long-term care insurance. For those seniors who have served even one day in a time of war (thank you for your service!), they may qualify for VA benefits, and oftentimes, their spouses will also qualify. Then there is Medicare, which is administered through the state. The average cost of assisted living care in America today is $4,500 per month per person, though that varies across states and cities. To find the average rates in your area, check out www.genworth.com/costofcare and search for your city or zip code.

Don't get me wrong; assisted living is expensive. But I urge you to think of it a little differently. How much does it cost you to live each month? Think about it: the food, the mortgage or lease, the fun, the cars, the activities, the utilities, everything. Now, what if you had a private chef, someone helping you with your daily hygiene, and someone doing your laundry and cleaning your house daily? It adds up pretty quickly, and $4,500 doesn't seem so bad anymore. My brother jokingly said when my dad got into this industry that it would be cheaper for him to move into the Residential Assisted Living home than for him to stay at his own home. It sounds pretty enticing to me!

The reality is that the cost of care is expensive, and no matter how we chop it up, only certain people will be able to afford it. I'm only sharing average numbers; what we focus on at Residential Assisted Living Academy is above-average homes and locations. But many seniors cannot afford average care homes, let alone above-average ones. For the seniors who need more support, the government provides some with Medicare/Medicaid at about $1,800 per month per person. Some assisted living homes and facilities will accept this amount. Unfortunately, the level of care, the quality of the food, and the size and style of the home reflect those lower numbers.

One of our students, Hal, was so eager to get into the business that he purchased the first RAL home he saw for sale in Phoenix, Arizona without using what he learned from our course! The average rates within the home were around $2,000 per month, and most residents were using government funding. With 10 residents, he was barely breaking even. He wasn't making enough money to provide them with daily activities or good quality food. He felt terrible and really hated that experience. So, he purchased another, more upscale home in Scottsdale and started cash-flowing really well. He decided to use those profits from the upscale home to help accommodate for extras at the lower-end home. This was a beautiful opportunity for Hal to give back to the senior community. Many of you may have a similar passion to give back and serve the underprivileged seniors of your community. By creating a cash-flowing home, Hal was able to provide services for seniors who otherwise wouldn't have been able to afford that level of care.

MYTH #8:

IT'S IMPOSSIBLE TO FIND AND KEEP GOOD EMPLOYEES

Our final myth to debunk is about finding and keeping excellent employees in a world where it seems no one "wants to work" and it's hard to find "good labor." *Invest in people and they will stay loyal!* Thinking that you will have a hard time finding people to work for you and stay with you is a limiting mindset frame. You're doubting yourself before even trying. What if you stopped doubting and started creating a beautiful RAL home where caregivers chomped at the bit to get a job? What if you had staff who begged to come in on their days off or pick up extra shifts? What if you had an administrator or manager who ran all of the day-to-day and who felt empowered and honored to carry your business into the future? What if you were creating jobs and giving people dignity back?

The future is in your hands. One of my favorite parts of this industry is finding the right people to work with you on your team. You can create a community and family environment where people are excited to come work and care for the residents. Our students, Jamie and Dana, in Alabama shared with me a beautiful story of their caregiver, whom we will call Kim. Kim LOVED the seniors in their home. She was so patient, kind, and thoughtful in her interactions with them. She was truly a five-star caregiver. But there was one resident who didn't like Kim and wouldn't do what she asked her to do.

Dana went to speak with the resident because she was confused. Kim was her best caregiver, and the resident didn't have issues with any of the other caregivers. What was it about Kim that was rubbing her the wrong way? Dana learned from the resident that she thought that because Julie didn't smile at her, she must be mean. She was happy to do whatever anyone wanted as long as they smiled. It seemed like a simple solution!

Dana quickly grabbed Kim and shared with her the information she had just learned. Kim looked down at the ground, shuffled her feet, and said, "Ms. Dana, I don't smile because I am embarrassed. I don't have my front teeth, and my smile is scary, so I haven't smiled since I was a little girl. Can someone else help the resident? I don't want to upset her. I love the resident. I just can't smile." Dana's heart shattered. She had no idea that Kim had been embarrassed about her smile. Her teeth had nothing to do with her work ethic, her heart, or her ability to connect with the residents and the families. It hadn't crossed her mind that this might have been holding Kim back. Dana told her she understood and would follow up.

Later that night, she asked Jamie what he thought about arranging dental work for Kim. Without hesitation, he agreed. Not only would the resident be happier to work with Kim when she had a shift at the home, but it would also help Kim to live her life more fully if she could smile without being embarrassed. It was the least Dana and Jamie could do as her employer. They made some appointments with a local dentist, and the next day, they brought Kim into the office. They told her how proud they were of her for sharing her struggles and how much they admired her work ethic, and how she truly was a star team member to them. They then told Kim that they had made her appointments to get veneers to take care of the missing teeth and that it was all paid for; all she had to do in return was… smile! Kim broke down in grateful tears. She had been hiding her smile for 20-plus years and never had enough money to fix them. Dana and Jamie's kindness and understanding was above and beyond. She is a loyal, devoted member of the team, and now she smiles all day, every day!

***

By this point, you have a good understanding of why owning a Residential Assisted Living (RAL) home is an amazing opportunity to do good and do well, and you know whether this type of investment is the right fit for you. So, how do you get started? In Part 2, we will explore the four ways to establish the perfect home and the pros, cons, and unique considerations of owning a home in your area vs long-distance ownership. In Part 3, we will talk about the three methods for funding your RAL, and in Part 4, we will take a deep dive into all the basics of filling your home with employees and residents. After reading this book, you will have a solid foundation for starting and operating your home, and if you are interested in taking it to the next level, Part 5 describes all of the amazing education, resources, and support that the RAL Academy has to offer. You can visit https://residentialassistedlivingacademy.com/ at any point to learn more about our proven formula or to sign up for a free introductory course, virtual trainings, or one of our live 3-Day Fast Track trainings.

PART 2

Find It

CHAPTER 6

Finding Your First Residential Assisted Living Home

There are four different methods for starting your own Residential Assisted Living (RAL) home (we'll explore each of these more in-depth in the following chapters):

Method #1: You can purchase land and build a custom RAL home from the ground up. This option could take the longest, but the home is most suitable for seniors. We've had many students do this, and I love this option if you live in an area where land is available. It's a very cool way to create a custom home that perfectly suits RAL needs.

Method #2: You can purchase an existing single-family home and renovate it for RAL. This is a great place to start, especially if you find a home that's almost suitable as-is; minor renovations can make a major difference. Generally, the rule of thumb is 300 to 500 square feet per person, so if you're planning to have 10 people, homes with 3,000 square feet should be the minimum in your property hunt. My father's second and third RAL homes were created using this method.

Method #3: You can purchase an existing RAL home, buying both the real estate and the business. This is the fastest and easiest way to get involved in the industry. It may cost a bit more upfront, but you're in the door ASAP. For my father's first RAL, he purchased an existing home and jumped in right away, two feet first!

Method #4: You can partner with someone and either (a) lease their home to run your RAL facility or (b) own the home and lease it to

someone else who runs the RAL facility. This is another speedy way to get started. Keep in mind, though, that you are in partnership with someone, so make sure you are ready and prepared for all that might entail. This method is what we are currently doing with our homes; we own the properties, and we lease them to someone to run the business. This is an extremely hands-off approach, which gives us the ability to invest in lots of projects all across the country.

Now, some people want to choose one option to just get started and help narrow their focus, while others are open to whatever opportunity comes their way. Both options are great, and it just depends on what feels right to you. Next, you need to determine where you're going to do this; are you planning to open a home close to where you live or further away? There are advantages to both approaches, and we'll dig into this more in Chapter 11. Once you know your answers to (1) whether you want to start with a specific or flexible approach and (2) whether you want to stay close to home or look further out, you can start refining your search.

Overall, no matter which of the four options you choose to take, the best advice I can give is to be open to opportunity! Whatever presents itself is what you should be ready and excited for. When you limit what you're willing to do, you limit your chances of success. RAL is so different from other types of real estate investing sectors because it's really best for someone who wants to make a difference in the world. This isn't just more tenants and toilets; it's an opportunity to make an impact and change lives while cash-flowing like you never have before on a single-family home.

MEMORY CARE HOMES VS. TRADITIONAL HOMES

There are two different types of RAL homes. First, there are homes for people who primarily have physical limitations, but their minds are sharp. Then there are memory care homes, which focus on providing care to seniors who suffer from pronounced cognitive decline due to diseases such as dementia and Alzheimer's. Most memory care homes charge an additional $500 to $1,500 per person per month because of the extra requirements that are involved with the additional staffing, licensing, and physical accommodations. If you live in a state where the rates are very low, the maximum number of residents is between six and eight, or the cost of living is super-high in general, memory care may be something to consider! These factors can help counterbalance a difficult state or city or market in general. In our 3-Day Fast Track training, we have incredible educators who teach on the subject of memory care and the differences between opening a memory care RAL home and a traditional RAL home.

A memory care home physically looks different due to increased precautions around resident safety. There are usually features such as different locks on the doors and a gate blocking the kitchen. Staff require a higher level of licensing and are typically paid more. Also, residents are typically much more mobile and are able to participate in physical activities at a vastly greater scale than in a traditional home.

In Dallas, Texas, our student, Loe, has five incredible memory-care-focused homes where the residents can often be found doing yoga, painting, and playing piano. It's a beautiful thing! This kind of home presents an interesting juxtaposition to our RAL homes, where physical movement is a struggle but conversations are flowing. The level and type of care in these homes is a game-changer. The love, time, effort, and hearts of everyone working in and owning these homes has to be top-notch. Last year, we hosted an incredible in-person memory care focused training (for those who want to learn more, you can head to www.residentialassistedliving-academy.com/memory-care. If you have a passion for helping those who are dealing with dementia or you want or need to have higher-than-average rates because of a difficult market, consider memory care as an opportunity that could meet your needs.

Before opening your first RAL home, make sure to research what already exists in the area. You can go to www.RALhomelocator.com, which is a directory of RAL homes across the country. When you open your own

RAL, you add your top-notch home to the map so we can help promote yours. If there are no care homes in your area, that may be a prime place to start your first one—less competition! But don't worry. Even if there are many homes in your area, the demand is still higher than the supply, so you can make it happen. And we can teach you how to set yourself apart from the rest.

CHAPTER 7

Method #1: Finding Land and Building Your Custom Home

The pros of finding land and building your own RAL home are that you can customize it to suit all of your needs. However, the cons are that it may take more time than the other options, so if you'd like to get your home up and running quickly, building a custom home might not be right for you. For those of you who are interesting in going this route, these tips will set you on the path to success!

Do your homework on state rules and regulations. Let's say you decide to do a custom build in your home state. Fabulous! Now you need to search for the land and determine the rules for building custom RAL homes in that particular area. The state-by-state rules and regulations can guide you, but really, it's up to you when you are doing residential or commercial custom builds. Our students, Brad and Angie, built custom RAL homes from the ground up in Kansas, and they are stunning! The state required them to add some components that felt pretty commercial, like a parking lot that could fit eight cars. While the home may not feel particularly residential when you pull up, the inside is a dream home. Sometimes, you have to adjust your vision to meet the legal requirements, but that doesn't mean you can't do it and should call it quits. If you need help finding your state's rules and regulations, schedule a discovery call with our team at www. RAL101.com so we can show you how to find those.

Before you purchase land and begin building your home, do your research. It is vital that you really optimize the perfect location. You need to determine what works now, what will likely work in three to five years and even in 10 to 15 years, because all of those time frames matter. Finding that demographic research and determining if it will stick or move is vital. Research big-box facilities in the area to determine how many beds are already available. Look into whether any other large facilities or corporations plan to come to that area in the next five years. All of this will help you determine if it's a good location or not.

Take full advantage of the benefits that a custom build has to offer. Building a custom home allows you to differentiate yourself from the competition. Make a movie theatre or a salon or a cool feature that none of the other homes in the area have. If it's custom, make it custom, and do something new, fresh, and different to separate yourself from the bunch. One of our students, Marcus, added an incredible feature to his custom-built RAL home in Arkansas: a home gym! He has a memory care home, and because he knew that his residents would more than likely be physically active, he thought he could combine his love of fitness and passion for helping seniors by adding some fun features. He has bikes, treadmills, weights, yoga mats, a mirrored wall, and a ballet bar. And better yet, he added a pickleball court to his backyard. Now that truly sets him apart and makes Daughter Judy say, "Wow!"

Stick to your timeline. We all know the old saying that whatever the contractor tells you in terms of timeline and cost, double it. But here's the thing: in this scenario, NO! Don't allow it. Shop around and find a contractor who will commit to timelines with incremental pay decreases for things that take longer. You may not be able to afford to keep things afloat for an exorbitantly long timeline, so it's vital that you play a hands-on role in making sure the project is completed on time.

Avoid overbuilding and overspending. Avoid the temptation to keep adding and adding. Yes, go for quality with flooring and features that will last, but do not overextend yourself. Flooring in most RAL homes needs to be re-done every five to seven years anyway. Pick something nice but easy to clean. Don't choose all top-of-the-line features. Make a budget and stick to it. Also, keep the size of your home reasonable. Don't go too big! Each senior does not need 1,000 square feet per person. At some point, it becomes too big to manage. And remember that it might hurt to walk 200 feet from the bedroom to the kitchen, so please don't make them walk 2,000 feet to the bathroom. It's too much to ask.

After you purchase the land and start building, you need to start marketing right away. This is very important. You must, must, must start marketing ASAP. This will help dramatically when the time comes to open the doors and start accepting residents. As soon as you find that incredible administrator who will oversee the day-to-day operations, hire amazing caregivers, and get the home inspected and licensed, you will be ready to host your first open house and welcome those new residents with open arms and hearts!

CHAPTER 8

Method #2: Purchasing and Converting an Existing Home

Before you start searching for a house to turn into an RAL home, do your research! First, you'll want to start with the local and state regulations. Some states have rules on specifics such as how far away one group home can be from another group home. Once you find an area that checks all of the legal boxes, you're ready to find the perfect house to convert into an RAL home!

Know your area. If you plan to convert a single-family house into an RAL home, then you should start by researching all the other homes in the area on www.RALHomeLocator.com to determine if you should purchase in that area. Is it overpopulated with homes, or is there a gap that you could help fill?

Find a home that needs minimal work. You're looking for a house that is already on its way to becoming your RAL home. For example, you would not want to choose a home that is 2,000 square feet if you are planning to have 12 residents. Using our rule of thumb of 300 to 500 square feet of living space per person, you would need a minimum of 3,600 square feet, preferably 6,000 square feet. With any house much smaller than that, the amount of renovation you would have to do would be substantial. So, if the initial home is only 2,000 square feet, then aren't the others in the neighborhood probably the same size? Yes! So that means that it's probably not the ideal place for your home.

Search for homes in well-populated, affluent areas. You want to find the places that have twice the median income with a large population of

Daughter Judys. In other words, your target area has a large number of people aged 50 to 70 years old who will likely be looking for long-term care for their parents and who can afford assisted living. And you want to avoid going too far away from civilization. Just because Grandma lives over the river and through the woods in the storybooks doesn't mean this is a good place to put your RAL home!

If at all possible, avoid neighborhoods with Homeowner Associations (HOAs). While you can certainly own an RAL home in a neighborhood with an HOA, it saves you a lot of headaches if you can skip this complication. Is it worth the fight? Not if you can avoid it!

Our student, Connie, decided to purchase and convert an existing home to an RAL facility in New Mexico. She found a 4,000-square-foot house and did all of her demographic research to make sure it was the right fit. The home needed only minor renovations: building out the garage into another bedroom, adding a small wall to the large secondary living room to create two bedrooms, and adding one bathroom. Adding bedrooms is always easier than bathrooms, so keeping those additions to a minimum was smart. She began her project and finished it to completion within five months; 10 days later, she hosted her first open house. Within three days, she moved in her first resident! Connie is a perfect example of what following this method can look like: starting with the proper demographics, not going crazy with the renovations, sticking to timeline and budget, being ready to open ASAP, and moving in residents pretty much as soon as the doors are open. Woohoo!

If you are not experienced with renovations or major additions for RAL-style homes, don't fret. We have floorplans available for purchase for our most advanced students.

CHAPTER 9

Method #3: Buying an Existing Residential Assisted Living Home

Buying an existing Residential Assisted Living home is generally the fastest and easiest way to get into the industry. The downside is that opportunities may be limited due to short supply. However, if you find the right opportunity, the benefits are many: the home is already in operation, you don't have to fill the beds or hire the staff, and you don't have to wait until renovations are done. You are moving and grooving immediately! My father got started in this industry by purchasing an existing home, and so do many of our students. It's a great way to get your feet wet and learn the industry. Then, if you want to explore other methods, you have a solid foundation of experience and understanding. That's the beauty of RAL investment. No one is holding you back. It's all about what you're open to and what makes sense for you.

If you take this approach, you will start by identifying all of the existing RAL homes in your area, visit the homes and the areas, and see which ones you would be interested in. Once you have your finalized list, here is what you are *not* going to do: barge in and ask right out of the gate if they are selling! Start building a relationship with the owner, and when the timing seems appropriate, discreetly raise the question about whether they might be interested in selling.

Here's an opening line that tends to work like a charm: "Hey, I am getting into the Residential Assisted Living industry. Do you know of anyone who might be selling their home? I may be interested in buying the business and real estate from them." This completely disarms them. You are not asking them directly, nor are you asking to see numbers. You're just searching to see if they know of someone. This type of question opens up the door to a conversation. They may connect you with someone who is looking to sell, or they may share with you that they are intrigued with what you have to offer.

Now the real negotiations and conversations begin. As with any business purchase, it's worth what someone is willing to pay. Don't be the one who overpays. The business is worth something, that's for sure, but having the financial suite—a tool our inner circle members have access to—can help you avoid major mistakes so that you don't overpay for a property that may not be worth it in the long run. If you are not well versed in evaluating a business, I highly recommend you come to our 3-Day Fast Track training, where we show you exactly what to look for and how to determine what you should pay to purchase these types of businesses. Also, finding the right realtor with experience who knows what to put in your contract is vital for this type of sale. Working with someone who knows what they're doing in the RAL world may save you a ton of time, energy, money, and stress! Make sure you've done your research on their reputation.

Always ask the person selling if they have multiple homes they would be willing to sell. Not only might you get a better deal, but we've had students, like Rick and Paul, who purchased a package of 10 homes at once. It all started with that first opening phone call. They did their research, identified existing RAL homes in the area, called the owners of the homes, and asked if they knew someone willing to sell. On their 30th phone call, DING DING DING! Not only was the owner willing to sell one home, he also had nine other homes he was looking to sell. Rick and Paul were shocked at how well this method worked and are an amazing example of how grit and perseverance can really pay off. You never know if the next caller might have exactly what you need. They were able to raise the funds to purchase this "10-pack" of homes, and now they're in the game in a big way!

Be aware that the owners who are selling may make false promises. Many will say that all of the staff will stay, the residents and their families are incredible, and everyone pays on time each month. All of these things may or may not be true. Don't listen to an owner who is desperately trying to sell, because they are more than likely sugarcoating things. We've personally had owners tell us they would hold our hands through everything for the first six months, and on day one, poof, they're gone! Sellers are not always going to be 100 percent forthcoming, and I want to prepare you to see through that. Take it all with a grain of salt, and let the numbers do the talking.

Once you purchase the real estate and the business, now you need to reassure the staff you are not going to fire them. Make sure they know that you want them all to stay. Then you need to see if there are any minor changes you want to make to the home, such as changing out light fixtures, painting, or fixing up the landscaping. It's very hard to do major renovations to a fully active RAL home because you will disrupt the peace, and the residents and their family members will not be pleased with you. Don't purchase a home thinking you're going to completely change the kitchen on week one or you'll redo the flooring in the first year. That's not going to happen! The way to renovate a functioning RAL home is one room at a time, so when a resident passes on, you can renovate that one room before moving another resident in. I understand this is not ideal, but this is the reality you face when this is the option you choose. For larger renovations like a kitchen or living room, it's best to wait until you have no residents if it's that important to you. If you have multiple homes in the area, you could move the residents to one of your other homes for the one to two weeks you plan to do the work, but it's extremely disruptive, and the families may be unhappy.

CHAPTER 10

Method #4: Establishing a Partnership

Last but not least, establishing a partnership is a great way to get involved in this industry! We highly suggest you go through the "94 Questions Before Partnering" document we provide to all of our students at our 3-Day Fast Track before getting into a business relationship with someone for your first RAL. In this option, you could play either role: owning the real estate and leasing it to the operator or leasing the real estate and being the operator. Let's dive into both options to see which is most suitable for your needs.

If you are in the role of owning the real estate, you would have purchased and converted the house to an RAL home, similar to what we outlined with the second "buy and convert" method. Then, you apply for the license through the state and set up the contract with the operator you are leasing to. Make sure you determine who is in charge of what, put it in the contract, and detail it at length. For example, are you responsible for maintenance or not? That's up to you and how you establish that contract. The last thing you want is resentment over unclear expectations about who is supposed to take care of what. Contracts are your new best friend.

We suggest that, as the owner of the real estate, you set yourself up for the least amount of responsibility. You would be joining the group of almost one-third of RAL owners who are remote owners, meaning you wouldn't necessarily have to live near the home or even in the same state. In those cases, the less responsible you are for the home, the better. My neighbor, Glade, does this method for the nine recovery homes he owns in Phoenix and Scottsdale. He owns the real estate, renovated the properties to accommodate the needs of the residents, licensed them through the state, set up his contracts, and now leases them out to operators. He hasn't been on the properties in years and is just passively cash-flowing. This opportunity is what we call being a "preferred real estate provider." You're getting twice the fair market rent with a long-term, low-impact tenant with little to no maintenance. It's a win-win-win!

One of our students, Ryan, who came to our 3-day training, purchased a home in northern California. He bought a distressed property for a great deal, and being a fixer-upper type of guy, he was able to retrofit the property to be a perfect assisted living home. Then he and his family had a change of heart and wanted to get out of California and move to a farm in the Midwest! So, he started calling local care homeowners in the area, letting them know he was looking for someone to lease the property to. It was licensed and ready to go; he just wasn't interested in running the business part anymore. After making only 13 calls, he had five offers! He weighed all of the options, and our team collaborated with him on reviewing and finalizing the contract. Ultimately, he locked in an incredible deal with a local care homeowner at $8,500 per month in rent with a 5% increase each year and an option to apply that money toward a purchase at the end of their eight-year contract. Then, he and his family packed up, moved east, and now he's surrounded by chickens, pigs, and cows on his farm, passively cash-flowing over $2,000 each month, and he's not responsible for a thing! And the new owner added a beautiful property to his portfolio and is cash-flowing $15,000 monthly on that property. It's truly win-win-win.

If you are on the other side of the deal, you will be leasing from someone in Glade's or Ryan's position. You may want to work with someone in this regard if purchasing and renovating a property seems daunting to you. Instead, you work out the lease agreement with the owner or landlord, and you rent the property to run your RAL business. One of our students created an incredible company called A Better Way Realty, and that's exactly what they do: purchase and renovate the properties and lease them to our students.

Your role would be to find and hire your administrator, market the home, and establish policies and procedures, such as housekeeping rules and residency agreements. Your next step would be filling the home with residents while your administrator hires the caregivers and contractors. You can expect to pay two to three times the fair market rate, and you will probably want to negotiate a longer-term contract. You will likely want to sign the lease agreement for three, five, or even 10 years. You want to avoid having to relocate the business after one or two years, so locking it in for longer will make all parties more comfortable. You don't want them to kick you out just when you're getting up and running and thriving.

The owner of the property may want to increase the leasing rate by a certain percentage each year as you establish yourself more within your business. Sometimes they will even give you an opportunity to apply what you have paid toward purchasing the property at the end of the contract if you are interested, similar to the arrangement Ryan made with his operator. Alternatively, they may offer you the first right to purchase the home in the event that they sell the real estate in the future. There are many things to consider for this contract.

Make sure that your contracts are very comfortable for all parties involved. Do not sign something that doesn't make sense for you. Make sure it feels fair, and if you need a second pair of eyes on that contract, don't hesitate to schedule a call with our team at www.rall01.com. We want to make sure you're setting yourself up for success. And, at the risk of stating the obvious, avoid partnering with someone you dislike! You don't have to be best friends, but you want to make sure whoever you partner with is going to be a good partner in business and life. You're going to be spending quite a bit of time with this person, and you need to get along.

On the investor side of this type of method, getting just a few of these homes could help you reach your freedom number in a truly hands-off way. On the operator side, this is a great way to get involved in the industry with little to no money upfront. While this can be a great option, it can also feel overwhelming. Remember that we are here for you! Sign up for our 3-day Fast Track training at www.ralacademy.com/training. We are more than happy to help you navigate through this exciting opportunity.

CHAPTER 11
Local vs. Remote Ownership

One of the benefits of owning an RAL home is the flexibility. You can choose to invest in a property in your area or in an entirely different part of the state or country, and there are pros and cons to both options.

REMOTE OWNERSHIP

Being open to purchasing a property outside of your area can be a fantastic way to get started in an industry that may be tough in your particular market, and it opens up a lot of options. We always tell people to live where they want but invest where it makes sense. With remote ownership, you can benefit from being able to run your home in a less expensive market. Many of our students come from more expensive markets like New Hampshire, Washington DC, San Francisco, Los Angeles, and New York City. Not only may some of those markets not work very well for an RAL home, but they're also super expensive. It can be daunting when you see that average rates for each resident need to be at least $9,000 per month to make the numbers work. Of course, there are many people in those markets who can afford it, but sometimes—especially for your first RAL home—it feels better to do it in a less-expensive market with rates that feel like anyone could afford, such as Georgia, Oklahoma, Texas, Idaho, or Tennessee.

One of my favorite benefits of being a remote owner is the opportunity to have a second place you call home. Especially in the beginning of getting your business up and running, you will have to visit often and spend lots of time there until things settle and are able to be run more remotely. Once it is up and running, you can visit as much or as little as you like. When a student comes to our training and suggests that they are considering being a remote owner, my first question is usually, "Where do you want to visit often and have a second home?" For some students, it's about being closer to family. Stephen was living in Minnesota but had a daughter attending Arizona State University. Not only did he want to escape the cold weather, he also wanted a reason to come see his daughter more often. He purchased an existing facility in Arizona, and his remote ownership journey began with the added benefits of more time with his daughter and more pleasant winters.

Last but not least, a major benefit to being a remote owner is the fact that you will be able to be the most hands-off owner possible, mostly due to that fact that you have to be! When your RAL home is around the corner from you, the temptation to visit every week or even every day is right there. A quick check-in to say hello and see how things are going can add up to a significant amount of time and energy. And that's fine if it aligns with your vision. However, I have found that most students are NOT interested in buying themselves a new job.

In fact, most students tell me they want the opposite: an additional revenue stream, a retirement plan, and a legacy to pass down that requires as little hands-on responsibility as possible. There are competitors of the Residential Assisted Living Academy who teach and train how to own, operate, and live in your RAL home, but that is not the method we do or teach in our course. They will tell you it's impossible to be a remote owner, but that's because they are working harder, not smarter, and aren't using the methods I've shown you here. Instead of working in your business, you should be working on your business. The most important thing a CEO or owner can do is to think, not do. When you are the one doing everything, you are not empowering your team to grow and thrive on their own, which leads to being surrounded by incompetent people. That is the opposite of what we do. I want you to feel completely capable of owning remotely, whether that means being 45 minutes or 1,000 miles away. It is possible, and you CAN do it.

Now that we have talked about the pros, let's discuss the cons. There are things that can go wrong when owning a business, whether you are down the street or 2,000 miles away. If you don't live in the same area as your RAL home, you will have to book emergency flights to get to the house. You may get calls in the middle of the night. You will have to have LOTS of communication with your staff. You will worry about things being handled differently than you would handle them. This is all part of being a remote owner and part of being a business owner in general. This new business is your new baby; it's important to raise it up right!

One of the major downsides to remote ownership is having less control, especially when significant events happen such as a staff member quitting suddenly or a severe maintenance issue. Related to staffing, we have a ton of tips on how to be the best remote owner possible to help mitigate issues like these, including ways to keep your staff happy so they are less likely to leave. However, things happen. First and foremost, we always advise all of our remote owners to prepare for specific situations, such as an administrator leaving unexpectedly. Your best protection is to have an assistant manager or assistant administrator on staff in case anything ever happens with the main administrator. That way, at least you have someone there who can step right in and fill their place until you hire a replacement.

You also need to have a full-blown accountability chart with an explanation of everyone's roles, clear expectations about who is responsible for what, and contingency plans in case someone is unable to fulfill their duties for any reason. Clear communication about each person's role and responsibilities is vital and is the foundation of your RAL's culture. When the team members know all of the policies and procedures within the home, including emergency and marketing plans, and understand the rationale behind them, it's much easier to swap staff and bring someone into the fold. So, if your manager walks out, you don't need to panic. You have an assistant manager who knows exactly what to do and a staff who is prepared to step up, and you will be ready to start hunting for the next lead manager position without missing a beat or needing to be on the ground yourself.

Related to maintenance, unfortunately these issues are unavoidable. Imagine that you live in Wyoming and receive a phone call from your administrator at 2:00 in the morning panicking because there was a severe storm that caused that roof to cave in, and now rain is pouring into the house. What are you going to do?! Well, first of all, we prepare our students for situations exactly like these. At the Residential Assisted Living Academy, we teach all owners, and especially remote owners, to have their list of contacts who are there to support the home in addition to backup options. This means having two contacts for any issue that might come up: chefs, landscapers, handymen, hairdressers, drivers, nurses, doctors, electricians, plumbers, roofers, painters, you name it. Think Noah's Ark—you need two of everyone! Having a strong relationship with your contractors is incredibly important. My father would treat all of our contractors like family, inviting them to the holiday parties, sending them small gifts and cards on their birthdays, and paying and tipping them generously. He would make sure they knew the story of the home and that if they had a loved one in the area who might need care, they would be welcome to come live in the home. The genuine connections and relationships are what get people to answer the phone at 2:00 in the morning for an emergency.

Going back to our caved-in roof scenario, what do you do? First, take a deep breath! You chose to be a remote owner to be away from the drama and the day-to-day, so it's expected that when you receive a call, it's likely an emergency situation. You're a business owner and a solution-maker; this is your time to shine. In a scenario like this, you need to set a calm tone, give your administrator immediate action items, offer your support, and reinforce your trust in their capabilities. When you're a remote owner, the administrator takes a lot of responsibility and ownership on their shoulders because you're not there to fill that role. They may feel an immense amount of pressure in a situation like this, and it's important to give them credit anywhere you can and let them know that you are proud of them. You may have to make last-minute trips on rare occasions when an emergency comes up, but generally, your administrator and staff will be fully capable of handling situations if you set yourself up for success.

One key ingredient to setting yourself up for success is setting boundaries. Keep in mind that, as a remote owner, you will have less control. It's the name of the game! You choose to be remote probably because you wanted to be hands-off, so in turn, you will have less say in the decisions and even less say in the day-to-day. This can be a pro and a con. When you have less control and something happens, there could be long-term issues. For example, let's say the manager has a tour with a family who says they can only pay $5,500 per month for their resident, but the room they're looking to move Mom into is set at a base of $6,250 per month. Instead of calling you, the manager just accepts the resident. Now, your manager may have all the best intentions and valid reasons for making this decision, but when you discover that most of your residents are paying $500 to $1,000 less than you have initially set rates for, this is a problem.

To prevent these issues, create a list with three columns: things that they can make decisions on without asking you or even telling you later, things that they can make decisions on but you want to be told about later, and things that they cannot or should not make decisions on without consulting you. Laying out these three categories and communicating about them from the beginning is life-changing as a remote owner.

Your lists may look something like this:

Things you can make decisions on and not tell me about:
- Changing who is coming to do activities with the residents that day
- Hiring or firing caregivers
- Buying items for the home under $1,500

Things you can make decisions on and please tell me later:
- When a new resident moves in or passes on
- An issue with a family member that you handled
- Issues with any contractors
- When the state comes for inspections

Things I prefer you do not make decisions on without talking to me:
- Major maintenance issues
- Family threatening to sue
- Purchases over $1,500

It's important to remember that things in these columns shift over time as you build trust with your administrator. In the beginning, you may have everything in the first column. Then as time progresses and you start to feel like you do not need to know every time someone shows up late to work, categories can shift to different columns. The key is talking through those shifts together. The more you build trust, the more things fall to the bottom categories, and eventually, you're only getting those "the roof has caved in" calls, which is what you're aiming for as a remote owner.

When it comes to the daily drama, it's out of your hands, literally; there is nothing you can do from Colorado when the home is in Arkansas! You have to trust your staff and trust that they're making the best decisions. You have to build a strong relationship with the administrator and the assistant manager. You also want cameras in the house. With these things in place, it's all you can really do, but it also can give you peace of mind. You can incorporate things like weekly or biweekly all-team Zoom calls, so the staff get to see your face and know your voice. So, when you text or call them to say that you hear they're doing great, you're not just a complete stranger. Not having to deal with the daily drama can bring a lot of relief.

Being a hands-off RAL homeowner takes time, practice, and lots of organization! It's vital for you to have all your ducks in a row: charts; graphs; policies; procedures; systems; documents; team training; culture reset meetings; coaching; and—maybe most importantly—patience. We are here to help if that is the route you plan to take with your new business. It's what we do and what we love to show our students how to do! One of my favorite parts of our training is when our staff comes to town. We have over 10 students who became RAL homeowners and eventually became staff members who teach at our 3-Day Fast Track trainings. Each and every one of them has the ability to completely shut off their phone and dedicate their complete focus on the event and the students. They never have to run out of a session to fix a problem at their home, because they successfully set up their businesses so they have the ability to walk away for days at a time and know that everything will be okay. Almost one-third of all RAL homeowners are remote owners; if they can do it, so can you!

LOCAL OWNERSHIP

There are also pros and cons to being a hands-on, in-town, local owner. One of the major downsides is that it's really hard to not visit the home all the time! When you're a small business owner, no matter the type of business, it's kind of like the business is your baby… so it's hard to fight the temptation to go check on your baby all the time. This makes it challenging to find that out-of-sight, out-of-mind headspace.

Also, you may struggle with feeling like you can do certain things better, which leads to you stepping in and starting to run things. We find this happens with our type-A students who run homes close to where they live. For example, on one of their visits they might observe a tour being given to a family and notice something they would have said differently or would have added. Even if the family chooses the home, they tell the administrator, "Next time you have a tour, call me and I'll do it," and they are jumping right back into the business. They are working *in* the business instead of *on* it, the opposite of what we want them to do!

There are plenty of advantages that come with being close to the home. If anything goes wrong, you can pop right on over without much inconvenience. And you will know everything happening in your business: when people are hired or fired, when there are tours, who's staying in the home. Plus, it can also be easier to market and recruit new residents because you won't be relying 100 percent on online marketing or your administrator. You will know people in the area and have connections, including friends who may be looking for a home for their aging parent.

Another benefit is that you will be able to meet and greet the families of the residents and can really build connections with the residents and the staff. If your heart is for seniors and you really love this industry, this might be the right option for you. We have many students who love that this is now their new "job." They are super involved in the day-to-day and they enjoy it immensely. For example, our student, Micah, is a registered nurse, and he started his RAL home with the intention to work as the administrator in the home. He was overworked and underpaid and very disturbed by the hospital environment he had been working in for over 12 years. He was ready to make a big change and to positively impact his community. This opportunity blended so well with his heart for the elderly. He loves spending his days with his staff and residents and touring the families through his property. To create some balance, he has hired two assistant administrators so he can take time off when needed. But he started this investment with the vision of being hands-on.

Another student, Sue, really enjoys cooking, so she is the chef in her RAL home! She goes over every morning to cook the seniors a made-to-order breakfast, goes grocery shopping, comes back, makes lunch and a dinner that can be reheated later, and calls it a day. She loves cooking, her kids are out of the house, she has the time and energy, and she saves money from not needing to pay a chef. It's a creative way to be involved in her home regularly. Although she doesn't HAVE to do this, she likes to do it and it makes her happy to be in the home every day.

Even if you do live nearby, there are ways to set up the business as if you are remote or hands-off. We live about 45 minutes away from our three homes and run them in a remote owner, hands-off type of way. But truly, it's all up to you. You have to decide what role you want to play. Remember: this is your business, and you have to set it up the way you want. We have many students who say that they will start by being more hands-on to save money. But we've found that there are two problems with this. First, they are not used to this kind of work, and they burn out quickly. If they don't burn out, then the second problem is that it's very hard for them to ever truly step away. Don't start doing something you don't want to do for the foreseeable future. Nothing is forever, but it's a lot harder to stop doing something after you see how it's saving the business money, how you do it best, etc. If you want to be hands-off, start and stay hands-off, and if you want to be hands-on, start and stay hands-on. It's all about the procedures, the strategic hires, and the way you cast your role and stick to it!

PART 3

Fund It

CHAPTER 12

Ways to Fund Your Home

You've decided that you want to invest in a Residential Assisted Living (RAL) home. That's wonderful! Once your home is up and running, you'll be making money to cover your costs. But when you first get started, you need a way to fund your new investment. The amount of money you'll need to raise will vary depending on which of the four options you choose and the prices in your area.

First, if you're choosing to build a custom home from the ground up, this will require a large investment of time and money. Usually, this includes the cost of the land, structure, and furnishings and at least two months of carrying costs after opening to give you time to fill the home with residents. Students have spent as little as $700,000 and upwards of $2.5 million using this route, so there is quite a bit of variability depending on the area. Overall, the homes that I've seen our students build from the ground up are some of the most beautiful RAL homes I have ever seen, so it is worth the investment if you are in a position to do so.

Second, if you're planning to renovate a single-family home into an RAL home, you'll need to raise capital to cover the cost of the real estate, the renovation, the furnishing, and the carrying costs for two months minimum. This is very similar to the funding with the first method, but you have more options related to how you pay for it. One of the cons with this method is that sometimes you have to work with what you've got when it comes to the renovations. For example, some HOAs do not allow the home to look different from other homes in the neighborhood, so you may have some restrictions to work around. However, it's not a deal breaker. This is actually the most popular method among our students, and they have spent as little as $150,000 and upwards of $1 million.

Third, purchasing an existing RAL is the fastest way to get started typically and has fewer categories of cost, which primarily consist of the business and the real estate. So, while you're saving on the cost of building, renovations, and furnishings, you're spending more money for the work that has already been done for you. You may need a small amount of capital to carry over, but the home should be 80 percent to 100 percent full upon time of purchase and should be cash-flowing already. However, there may be some fallout from past staff or residents, so you always want to protect yourself and your investments. Better safe than sorry! With this option, costs can range from $500,000 to $3 million depending on many factors.

Lastly, you could lease a home to use for your new RAL business. In this case, you are spending a lot less money upfront typically, depending on who's leasing to you. They may ask for one to two months of lease payment upfront or a small lock-in price fee to show that you're serious. But mostly you're just going to need finances to cover the furnishings and carrying costs as you launch your business. You should always overestimate costs when making financial plans with your investors. The worst thing you could do is to go back to them and ask for more money. That isn't a good look and is a sure way to get people to never want to work with you again. This method is the cheapest in terms of upfront costs, typically less than $500,000.

All of the options above require you to cover carrying costs, which refers to all of the monthly expenses that need to be "carried" while the revenue or income isn't meeting the expenses just yet. So, for example, if your home is going to cost $28,000 per month to run, you'll want to prepare for about $60,000 in carrying costs (two months' worth). This is important because you need to pad yourself. You probably won't need all of it if you are marketing correctly and have done all of the recommended steps, but this will be crucial in times of need. Typically, you might need to cover about 50 percent of the first month's expenses, 25 percent of the second month's, and only 10 percent of the third month's. Setting aside enough to cover 100 percent of bills for the first two months is just a good rule of thumb to give you some buffer room for the first few months as you fill your RAL with residents and get everything up and running.

One of the most common mistakes new owners make is completely furnishing all of the bedrooms. In most states, you only need to furnish a few bedrooms at first, because as seniors move in, they will bring some of their own items and will start to fill the room themselves. For example, if you have a 12-bedroom home, you should fully furnish five of those bedrooms with beds, dressers, nightstands, lamps, TVs, etc. Over time, every room will eventually be furnished with a mix of the things you bought and the things the residents have brough over the years. If you furnish all 12 bedrooms in the beginning, you will end up paying for storage! This is one of those tips that doesn't seem important… until it is. We cover all of these tips and tricks in our trainings to help students avoid expensive mistakes and set them on the path to success.

Regardless of which build option you choose to get started, there are many ways to raise capital for your RAL home. There are plenty of people who are looking to invest but don't know who to invest with or what to invest in. They need help, and you may be the right person to "help their money find more friends" as Mr. Wonderful from Shark Tank likes to say! Keep in mind that you may also have more untapped resources in your own pocket or backyard than you realize too. However, don't underestimate the power of OPM: Other People's Money. It is a great way to get started in this industry and it's right in front of you. You just have to show up prepared, open the door, and ask!

Overall, there are three easy ways to start raising capital right away. Please note these are specific results from certain examples and all situations vary. Consult with your accountants and lawyers before embarking on this venture.

The first option is working with investors. When I travel around the country, excited investors come up to me all the time and say, "Hey, I love what you're doing and I would be very interested in connecting with the best of the best from your class to hear about their projects. If it's the right fit, I'd love to personally invest with them." It's important to note this because too many people come to our training and have a terrible attitude about raising capital. They believe that it's impossible and that no one would want to lend to them, but that couldn't be further from the truth.

The second option is to get a loan. There are some loans that are an especially good fit for an up-and-coming RAL owner and home operator, such as a Small Business Administration (SBA) loan. In our training, we cover the top loans that our students like to call upon when starting their first homes. A loan can be a great way to get started in this business, and many times they will cover the cost of the home as well as the business startup and carrying costs. Keep in mind that you will want to review the specifics of the loan with a trusted advisor to make sure the terms are favorable for you.

The third option is to start by using your own capital. Some of our students come to us after inheriting or earning a large lump sum of cash that isn't necessarily safe or best to just hold on to, and they want to set themselves up to receive great returns. If you are someone who has money and needs to do something with it, RAL may be the perfect solution. Investing is an incredible way to protect your personal gains, and what could be better than letting your money work for you!

These three simple ways to secure funding to start your Residential Assisted Living journey are just the beginning, and we will explore each one more in-depth in the upcoming chapters. Truly, though, the options are limitless, and we cover the top seven ways to raise capital in our 3-Day Fast Track training. We have worked with students who have successfully used a variety of methods for raising capital, and we are always amazed by their creativity. When your passion and whys are strong enough, the grit kicks in. With investing and raising capital, don't forget: the return *of* the capital is always more important than the return *on* the capital!

CHAPTER 13
Finding Investors

Using OPM (Other People's Money) is a great way to start your first home, but the idea of finding investors who want to work with you can be daunting. Don't worry—we've got your back! We have been in this industry for almost a decade, and it's incredible what is out there when you know who to ask, where to go, and how to make the most out of your opportunity. It's important to avoid the money-hungry sharks and to work with investors who get what you do and who understand what value you will be providing. When you can explain the passion behind your project, you will open many ears, hearts, and wallets. I guarantee it.

With the RAL Academy on your side, you're going to do just fine. For our top-level students, or our inner circle students, we provide our curated list of names, emails, and phone numbers of private money lenders all across the country who are ready and excited to invest in this opportunity! They don't want to own the property or operate the business; they just want to lend out to our students and get a return on their capital. These three student success stories show just how feasible it is to find the right investors to start your business.

Alice started calling people on the Private Lenders List right after she finished her business plan. She was purchasing an existing business and needed to do minor renovations. It was already cash-flowing, so it wouldn't take much time for her to turn the house into what she hoped it would be. Alice needed to raise $1 million for the project total cost, and after a couple of weeks and many phone calls, she lined up three accredited investors who were all going to receive 12 percent back on their money over the course of five years. It was a great deal for everyone, and her hard work paid off. You have to be willing to do what it takes to get what you want. Alice is a perfect example of that grit and determination to get to the end goal. She was thrilled, and her investors were thankful for an incredible opportunity.

Winona was looking to raise capital for her custom-built RAL home. She started with the Private Lender's List and was pleasantly surprised when many investors opened their hearts and wallets to her project. She also received phenomenal feedback on her custom business plan. Bankers and investors alike were mega-impressed with her numbers and what she had planned. Within three months of taking the 3-Day Fast Track, she had locked in all the money she needed to get started, including carrying costs for the first six months, and she broke ground on her land just one month later!

Sometimes, the perfect investor is someone who is already in your life. Brad was sent to 3-Day Fast Track training by his father, who was very big in the tech world. After the training, Brad was excited to share with his dad how to get started in the business and what steps they needed to take. But Brad's dad wasn't going to let him off easy. He needed to see the numbers and to know that this was going to be a safe investment for him to make. So, he asked Brad for a business plan. Brad created his board of advisors, which included three of our RAL Academy industry leaders, and worked with us to pull together all of the numbers for his project. With everything over-the-top prepared, he went back to his dad to present the offering and make the big ask. His father was so impressed that he asked Brad for a second meeting with 10 of his tech-investing friends along. They all wanted a piece of the pie, and now Brad owns six homes in Chicago.

When you find the right investors, it truly is a win-win-win situation for everyone involved!

CHAPTER 14

Getting a Loan

When it comes to getting a loan, there are many routes you can take. Traditional bank loans have often worked for our students who just needed a small amount to get started, and that option might be a perfect fit for you. You can also work with friends and family to negotiate a personal loan.

A third option is to apply for a Small Business Administration (SBA) loan. However, be prepared for an oftentimes long and strenuous process. I have two pieces of advice for anyone applying for an SBA loan. First, start calling the local lenders you might be interested in working with early in the process, even if you have not yet identified a property you want to purchase. When you contact them and ask what you will need to apply for a loan with their company, they will usually give you a list of five to 20 items that they will need. Keep this list handy because you might not be ready to apply at that point and can use the information to start working towards checking off all the items on the list. This leads to my second recommendation: be ready and stay ready so that your loan process does not cause delays. Gather the list of what is needed and start getting it prepared now. Even though Noah didn't see rain, he still built the ark. Preparation is KEY! Get all your ducks in a row so that when you are ready to apply for the loan, you can pull it together, submit it, and push through the process much faster. Paying for speed, that's what we are all about.

Even though applying for an SBA loan can be a long, arduous process, students who take our trainings have the extra benefit of building connections that will make everything smoother and easier than you can imagine. In our training, you learn about the top companies to work with and the top companies to avoid, and we help you find the best lenders in your area. I can't wait for you to come to our class and discover all of this incredible information; it's truly going to help you to soar!

Our student Monty from South Carolina needed a loan for his project and decided to use one of our preferred SBA lenders. He was able to lock down $3 million to buy land and build two custom RAL homes on one lot. Another student, Camille, used an SBA loan to start her homes in Georgia. She called one of our preferred vendors immediately upon leaving the 3-Day Fast Track training and asked what she needed to prepare. They gave her the list, and she got started right away. Camille gathered her documents and worked with our team to create her custom business plan, pro forma, and projections. She found her desired property and called the SBA lender back as soon as she was ready. She submitted all the required paperwork and got moving right away. They were able to lend her $900,000 for her project, which allowed her to renovate the property, furnish the home, and hold over the carrying costs until she was full.

If you're not using your own money, what's stopping you? Nothing stopped Monty or Camille!

CHAPTER 15

Using Your Own Money

For some of you, raising capital is maybe not something that has crossed your mind because you have your own capital that you can use. That is perfectly acceptable, and I would love to share with you some stories of students who were able to do just that: invest in themselves and use their own capital to get started.

We have a wonderful student named Demetri who had recently lost his father and inherited $4 million. He came to our training because he wanted to invest in something new and exciting. His father had suffered from Alzheimer's, and Demetri thought opening a home that focused on memory care would be a beautiful way to honor his father's legacy. He used about $1.5 million of that money to purchase land in Nevada and start building a custom home from the ground up. The home is stunning and serves 12 residents with memory care issues now. He was able to fund the entire project out of pocket and is now making great returns.

You may be in a situation where you have capital that came to you suddenly and you are looking to protect your assets or to put that money in a safe investment. Investing in yourself or someone who wants to do this business might be a smart choice. (Please note: I am not a lawyer or accountant, and you need to speak with your preferred parties to decide what is the best decision for your unique situation.)

There are a few potential pros and cons of using your own capital. Let's start with the pros. First, when you're not relying on someone else's money, you can get started much sooner. Second, you don't have to deal with the pressures to pay someone back and ensure they are receiving great returns. Plus, all of the great returns go directly back to you. Third, there may be tax advantages to investing in an RAL home, depending on your situation. As far as cons, one of the downsides is that you can't use the money for other things once you dedicate the funds to this project. It's 100 percent up to you and your advisors to determine what is the best option for your resources. Of course, you can always use some of your own capital and raise the rest or work with a partner to leverage their capital for the remaining portions needed. The sky is the limit, so be creative!

We have a lovely student, Mae, who was left with a large sum of money after her husband passed away. When Mae came to us, she was interested in learning more about how to start using her own capital to invest in an RAL home. One of her major concerns, though, was taxes. We sent her to an asset protection course with Don Pendleton from Protect Wealth Academy (protectwealth.com/ral). Don shared with her all the juicy details that the rich and famous use to protect their assets, and Mae was thrilled to know that she could invest in her own RAL home. She used her own personal capital to purchase an existing RAL business, and she was up and running right away. Impact investing is what most attracted her to this industry, and she loves to see the peace, love, and comfort her home brings to so many families and seniors.

Investing in yourself is key, and if you have the resources to fund your own projects and not have to deal with other parties, this may be a very attractive option. Not everyone has the capital to do this, and that's completely okay. Even if you do have the capital to completely fund your own project, you may prefer not to. Investing in RAL has wonderful returns, and the numbers have to make sense. If you are evaluating a deal and need extra eyes on it to make sure your money is going to be safe and secure, let us know. We are always here to help sort through those types of situations.

PART 4

Fill It

CHAPTER 16

Licensing

Now that you've found your home and secured funding, it's time for the exciting part: filling your home with residents and staff! But before you do, you first need to have your home licensed. Each state varies a bit on the specific steps to get licensed, so one of the first things you'll need to do is determine the rules and regulations of the state and county where you are choosing to start your Residential Assisted Living (RAL) home. Once you determine the rules, you can find the licensing form on your state's website. If you are unsure where to find your state's licensing forms, be sure to grab tickets to our next upcoming 3-Day Fast Track training. We have done all the hard work for you and have collected the rules, regulations, and licensing links for all 50 states, which we give to our students.

Many times, the licensing form requires information about the physical home, so you will need to have purchased or have signed a lease agreement on your RAL facility. Now, I know that may seem scary. What if the application gets denied? That is OKAY! There is no need to stress, since you can keep applying until you get it approved. You will have already done your due diligence to find a suitable property and research zoning before purchasing the home, so you will know with 100 percent certainty that the RAL home will work. You will have also followed all the state rules and made the recommended changes to the property, so the only thing missing is the state's approval with their licensing stamp.

Typically, the licensing form asks for generic information, such as the name of the company, address, number of residents, square footage, and level of care you plan to offer. Each state has a varied timeline on processing the paperwork. Regardless of your state, we always suggest you go straight to the office where you would be mailing or submitting the application online and instead directly hand it to the person in charge of processing the paperwork.

After you have submitted your application, the next step will be for the licensing office to send someone to the home to check that everything is in line with what you described in your paperwork and is safe for seniors. We recommend that you ask about arranging the home visit while you are in the office delivering the paper application. There is no harm in asking to be bumped to the top! You should work to befriend them and let them know you'll be back for more homes as you have grand plans to help the community.

Once the paperwork is approved, a state employee, a local fire marshal, or both will visit the property to do the home tour. They will give their stamp of approval and then you will wait for the paperwork to come back to you with the license and approval for however many beds they said yes to. Remember, your state rules and regulations are the best place to start to find all these items needed. What are the square-footage requirements? What are the rules on shared bedrooms and bathrooms? What are the rules on the windows and doors and points of egress? When you purchased or leased the property, you will have already done your homework and will have retrofitted the home to be suited for these needs. These are the exact details they are checking during the licensing application process.

At this point in the process, they will ask who the licensed administrator is. If it is not too difficult in your particular state to get a license as the administrator, we always advise that you get it. But if it's a very long and laborious process, then do not do it yourself. Hire an administrator as soon as possible. My father hired his first administrator on the day he closed on his first RAL home. Even though he had not applied for the license yet, he knew that key player was worth bringing on sooner rather than later. In some states, you may need to include your administrator's name on your licensing application.

If paperwork really isn't your thing, make sure you attend RAL Academy's 3-Day Fast Track so you can feel confident about and comfortable with the licensing steps. This will save you lots of time, energy, and stress. We love to coach our students through the entire process, from finding the home and doing the renovations to applying for licenses and hiring key players. These are all essential parts of starting your RAL business, and we can't wait to help!

CHAPTER 17

Hiring the Right Employees

When you set out to start a business, you may underestimate the importance of a team, but I'm here to tell you that in RAL, your team is VITAL! You must create and maintain a strong, united team. Those first few hires are essential to setting the tone for your new business. If you have never started a new business, this part can be challenging. If you would like to learn the best way to hire the right staff, I encourage you to snag your ticket to our next 3-Day Fast Track training. Overall, there are four key ingredients to the hiring process, including the Predictive Index test, core values, mission statement, and job descriptions, and four broad categories of positions you will need to fill, including the administrator, assistant manager, caregivers, and independent contractors. Retaining your staff is essential, so we will also review our proven strategies for keeping your team happy and fulfilled.

PREDICTIVE INDEX TEST

The key to hiring for your RAL is to find people who are a great fit both for working alongside you and for working with your residents in your home's culture. In the beginning, it will be important to lay out your house policies and procedures, identify what types of people you will need to hire and who you work best with, and set expectations around acceptable behavior, language, and work ethic. We highly suggest you take the Predictive Index test to find out your strengths and weaknesses as a leader and the CEO and Owner. This test will tell you a lot about yourself and how you naturally operate in business. Then, when you're ready to make a new hire, you can create a profile based on what you're looking for in that person. You can ask applicants to take a two-question quiz, and in conjunction with the findings from your test, their results will (a) indicate whether they are a good fit for the position and (b) provide a relationship guide for how the two of you will work together. This is gold! Ultimately, it will help save you time, money, and energy on hiring and training.

CORE VALUES

Another strategy to help with the hiring process is to write down your core values. What are things that are non-negotiables for you when it comes to someone's character and commitment within your business? For my father, his core values within his home were (1) creative thinking skills, (2) commitment to quality care, and (3) a fun attitude. These core values drove his hiring and firing decisions. He built his RAL home's team culture around these. If someone was not showcasing one of these core values, such as showing up to work each day with a poor attitude and bringing other team members or residents down, that was a fireable offense. He genuinely wanted people to enjoy coming to work and to love being a part of his team.

Don't know what your core values are? Ask yourself these two questions: Who do you admire or look up to in life, and why? Name three people and three reasons each. This exercise will reveal your core values. You might say, "My uncle Tom because he overcame addiction and put family first. He was brave and courageous and that just makes me so proud." So, one of your core values might be "family first" and another might be "bravery." Let's keep going. Maybe next you say, "My wife because she is so selfless. She always puts the kids and me first, and I just admire that so much in her. She's thoughtful and kind in all of her interactions, and when I come home from work, she drops everything to listen to me and comfort me." A core value then might be "selfless service to others." Next you might say, "My grandmother was a queen! She raised me and my brother, and wow, she really knew how to make us feel special. Her personality shone through every single day, and the way she would light up a room just made such a major impact on me. Being kind and fun-loving was her way of life." Altogether, your core values might be (1) family first and selfless service, (2) being brave, and (3) fun-loving. Let's translate these to professional values that will be the foundation of the culture in your RAL home and your hiring decisions.

Core Value #1: Putting others first

When you talked about your uncle, you admired the fact that he made sacrifices and changes for the betterment of your family, and when you talked about your wife, you highlighted her kindness and selflessness in taking care of others' needs. At work, this value might look like someone who puts others first, such as the residents, the team, the home, or the company.

Core Value #2: Honesty, transparency, and bravery in all interactions

Being brave is all about saying and doing the right thing even when it's scary. At work, that looks like caregivers being honest with you about things like whether they are happy in the home, if there are issues with any of the team members, and when mistakes are made.

Core Value #3: Positive attitude and fun is required

Last but not least is fun-loving. Most companies, homes, or people don't care if you have fun at work, but because you care, this will be something that draws in a specific audience. I mean, what are we doing in life if not having a blast, right?!

JOB DESCRIPTIONS

Now that you have your Predictive Index test results and core values, it's time to create great job descriptions for the roles you want to fill: a licensed administrator or manager, an assistant manager, caregivers, and any other independent contractors. Lay out your ideal vision for what each individual would do and be responsible for, and then compare your description to other job descriptions in the local area. Think about it from the applicant's perspective. If they are job-hunting and your job description has 1,000 things listed that they are required to do and the other home down the street has seven things, they may not apply to your business out of lack of understanding or feeling like they are not qualified. The next step will be to pare down your ideal list to be more realistic and approachable. Then, think about benefits and extras you may want or need to include. What are you planning to pay for these roles? What benefits may your staff have access to, if any? Are you competitive with other homes in the area?

Next, you will go back to your Predictive Index results, and you will create tests for those roles. Within the Predictive Index, you can create job profiles, so you will take a quiz based on the job description and answer the questions as if this is what you would expect from the applicant. If you can have two or three people do the same thing, you will build your ideal profile for your new role. If this sounds like a lot of work, we've got you covered in our 3-Day Fast Track training! We gave the Predictive Index profile quiz to the top 20 administrators and 40 highly qualified caregivers from across the country. Not surprisingly, the two roles mapped onto two to three preferred profiles. When our Inner Circle students are hiring, they can send their applicants the Predictive Index quiz and access our ranking system to see if the applicant falls into the correct category.

Our student, Sam, did this with three administrator applicants. After sending the applicants the link to the quiz, we did a coaching call with Sam to review the results. Based on Sam's personal profile and our ranking system, we suggested hiring applicant #2. Not only did that individual most closely match the preferred administrator profile but also had the personality and skills to get along with Sam best and cause him the least drama. Sam hired that person as his administrator, and they've been working together ever since!

MISSION STATEMENT

When it comes to creating your business's mission statement, ask yourself the following questions. What do you want your business to be remembered for? What does your business do? Why does your business do these things? Then start brainstorming. Get creative. Don't eliminate or cross out answers or stop yourself from writing them down. Just brain dump it all down and go crazy! You can incorporate other top-tier people who you know from your personal or professional life and who may have helpful input. Once you have a nice list of answers and feedback, it's time for refining. Cut out anything that doesn't sit right with you or that doesn't define your businesses and core values. Once you have those key elements, key words, and key phrases, it's time to review. This isn't about writing an essay. Keep it short and concise without being too limiting. Don't be afraid to change it. Once you feel like you have the core components down, present it to your closest circle for one final feedback and refinement session.

Here are two excellent examples of mission statements that may help you through this process. Warby Parker's mission statement is, "To offer designer eyewear at a revolutionary price while leading the way for socially conscious businesses." TED's mission statement is, "Spread ideas." Both of these are simple, clean, and to the point. You can easily see how they align with the answers to the core questions about what the business does and why they do it. Follow these guiding principles to create your own business mission statement for your RAL home.

Filling Positions

Now that you have the core values, the job description, the preferred Predictive Index profile, and the mission statement, you are ready to post the job online! You can post it to regular hiring sites such as Indeed, LinkedIn, even Craigslist, and you can also advertise in many other markets such as caregiver training schools, local newspapers, and placement agents and managers from other homes. You may even want to use a hiring service to help in the beginning.

Administrator

Your first hire is one of the most important people you are going to bring onto your team. The administrator will help with the rest of the hiring decisions, so it is immensely valuable to choose someone you know, like, and trust. They will truly be the face of your company, and you need to make sure that their core values align with yours. You will want to do your research on their experience in the industry and make sure they really grasp and understand your vision for your RAL home. If you own or plan to own multiple homes, you may not be hiring them to oversee just one home and instead need to bring them into the bigger picture. Whatever the vision is, be open and honest with them during the interview. Explain your story and your heart and connect with them. I always advise doing interviews in person not only because it helps with connection but also because their body language can be very informative.

Caregivers

Once you have locked in the administrator, it's time to find some caregivers! We always advise a five-to-one resident to caregiver ratio during the day and 10-to-one ratio at night, and their shift lengths impact how many caregivers you need to bring on board. For example, if you plan to have a 10-resident home, you will need two caregivers during the day. Since their shifts will be either eight or 12 hours depending on how you set up the schedule, they may only be working three to four days each week. This means you will need a minimum of six caregivers. Generally, I advise having a roster of at least 10 caregivers for a 10-person home, because this leaves buffer space for callouts, sick leave, or anyone quitting unexpectedly. Once you have more homes, you can share your staff between the homes. If your homes are owned under different LLCs, then you would not be paying overtime. In fact, it is common practice for caregivers to work two full sets of shifts at both homes. If a caregiver is only given work at your home three days each week, then they are more than likely working at another home down the road for the rest of the week. It's a mutually beneficial arrangement for you to have the same caregivers under your roof and for the caregivers to have consistency in their work.

Assistant Manager

When hiring for the assistant manager position, keep in mind that the perfect person might be one of the caregiver applicants. During interviews, I like to make sure we are mentioning that this position may be open to select persons who qualify and are a good fit. This will automatically make that potential candidate want your job more because they are already seeing growth potential! Don't promise anything, and make sure that this assistant is a good match for your administrator. For example, if your administrator is amazing at giving tours to the families but not so good at scheduling the caregivers' shifts, then be sure to build the assistant's roles around the administrator's weaknesses so they can balance one another out. If the administrator is great at hiring and firing staff and caregivers but not good at marketing the home, find an assistant who loves to market and has creative and fun ideas on how to get the word out about the home.

Pairing an administrator and assistant can be a tricky job, but it's so important to incorporate balance, background, and personalities to find that perfect fit. Keep in mind that someone may show that they are qualified over time. Sometimes you will find a caregiver who demonstrates a sense of ownership and pride that the others don't. They speak to the families with authority and respect, and they stand up for the core values and mission of the home. The assistant manager role does not need to be filled immediately, and sometimes the right person comes to you in unexpected ways.

Independent Contractors

Next, you will want to hire independent contractors, which may include nurses, doctors, activity coordinators, landscapers, chefs, roofers, hairdressers, and drivers, just to name a few. There may be a long of list people you are hiring as contractors to do all sorts of work around or inside the home. This is a list that you want your administrator to be involved in helping to build. More often than not, your administrator and their assistant manager will be the ones coordinating and working with these contractors, so making sure they are all clear on job roles and responsibilities is key. Creating visual charts on policies and procedures can be a helpful strategy for making sure that everyone is on the same page.

Once you've hired all the people for the open positions, make sure you are keeping your company culture alive. You can do this in many ways:

- Celebrating holidays, birthdays, and special events
- Helping employees achieve personal and professional goals
- Hosting weekly or monthly town halls or newsletters
- Creating a referral plan to offer bonuses for staff who bring in new residents
- Doing staff-of-the-month shout-outs
- Scheduling events like "Spin the Wheel Wednesdays" where staff can win small gift cards or prizes

There are many things to consider when it comes to keeping culture alive and well within the home. Don't let your mind be the limitation. You are building your very own RAL home, and it's up to you to set the standards you want to see come to life!

Retaining Staff

Even though finding and keeping staff can be a challenge in general these days, most of our students have no problems in this area. I recently spoke with one of our students in Connecticut about her experiences with staffing. Deirdre has had her RAL home for two years, and not a single caregiver has left. That seems crazy, right? She follows exactly what we teach: *invest in your staff and they will be loyal.* At our latest inner circle event, our students got together and shared their top tips for retaining their staff:

- Offering benefits: life insurance, 401k, flu shots, Costco memberships, gym memberships
- Providing paid time off
- Giving awards and superlatives at quarterly team meetings
- Offering internships for subjects that interest your staff
- Knowing their love languages and using love languages to give recognition
- Implementing profit share when the home is 100 percent full or there are no deficiencies
- Promoting from within, such as promoting an assistant manager from an existing home to a manager position when you open a new home
- Offering bonuses for referrals for other staff members or residents

- Team parties and Starbucks Tuesdays
- Asking for feedback and actually using and implementing it
- Inviting them to events where they can grow and expand their knowledge, like RAL National Convention
- Providing continuing education on RAL National Association's free membership site

All of these ideas may seem small, but they make a huge difference and set you apart from other facilities. The big-box homes do not care what the staff's love language is or how much effort they are bringing day in and day out. As RAL owners, we do care! One of our students, Matt, shared that, when he brings on a new staff member, he asks about their family and their life and career goals. He then makes sure to celebrate events like birthdays and anniversaries and has even provided scholarships for some of his caregivers to attend community college.

One of our students, Sylvia, helped a caregiver get their GED, and another student, Laura, actually bought a car for her manager when her car broke down. These things make our homes stand out! Can you imagine if you were that caregiver and your boss got you a scholarship to go to school? Can you imagine what kind of conversations you're having with your friends or family members about your job if your boss bought you a car when you were in need? Can you imagine how loyal and committed you would be to that job? These things are so much more important than paying $1 to $2 more than the next home. It's all about the culture and setting the tone that you are committed to them.

Of course, issues may arise with staffing. In those times, it's up to you to be a leader and help settle these issues to give the best outcomes to everyone involved. Having cameras in the common areas throughout the home can help solve many issues, and having a strong sense of culture will help these issues rise to the top. Most importantly, make sure that you and your administrator are in agreement about how to handle staff issues. In the beginning, you will likely be more involved in managing these incidents, and over time your administrator will understand and recognize what you want to happen. The goal is for the administrator to feel so confident and comfortable within their role that they solve the problems on their own.

Here's the thing to remember: when you hire the right staff and invest in them, your home will run smoothly. Of course, there are horror stories, but I guarantee that if you asked those owners if they did ALL of the steps above, their answer would be "no." There is no need to reinvent the wheel. Simply use our proven tools for the best results. When you follow the RAL Academy method, you will be able to trust that your staff can handle the most common issues that arise and that your residents feel cared for. After all, you are providing excellent job opportunities for the right people, and for that you should be proud.

CHAPTER 18
Finding Residents

Once your home is licensed and your staff is hired, it is time to fill your home with residents! Marketing is fundamental to this process and should start as soon as possible, even before your doors are officially open. This may sound counterintuitive, but it will take time to generate interest in your home, and you want to get up and running quickly. You also want to create a buzz around your new business so that when you do open, you are set up for success.

Over the years, we have found that these 10 marketing strategies help our students' homes stand out in just the right way:

1. Website

2. Facebook Page

3. Brochures and Flyers

4. Community Relationships

5. RAL Home Locator

6. Business Cards

7. Drive-by Marketing

8. Placement Agency Connections

9. Great Reputation

10. Testimonials

WEBSITE

You need to have a website that showcases contact information, videos, photos, and highlighted features that show why someone should choose your business. When we conduct surveys and ask our Daughter Judys what they are looking for in a Residential Assisted Living home website, they almost always say location, price, and amenities. If you can include a starting price on your website, that can be a nice touch to set you apart, since many facilities will not put pricing on their sites. Adding a map with your location and what you are close to in the area helps families visualize where their loved one would be living. Amenities will be an important quality-of-life consideration and will distinguish you from other places.

Having a good-looking website will get you some home tours that you didn't expect. Having no website will turn away many people. We live in the digital age. People want to research as much as they can about you before they set foot in your home. In this industry, having no reputation can be just as damaging as having a bad reputation.

Check out some of our incredible students' websites:

https://estrellagardens.com – This website is not only aesthetically pleasing, but it also has many nice touches that set it apart from the average website. It has a quiz to start going over what level of care your loved one might need and features a cost calculator to determine an estimate of fees for the care and stay. It also has a stunning video that showcases the home and a list of the featured amenities and services within the property. Finally, it ends with frequently asked questions (FAQ). The website is approachable and educational and helps to address concerns that come up when someone is considering placing their loved one or parent in an RAL home.

https://meetseasons.com – For a professional vibe, I love this website. It feels incredibly clean and fresh. The green coloring and the logo are simple and comforting. One particularly unique feature that I love about this site is the information at the bottom of the home page: number of residents served, number of families helped, years of service, and testimonials. This helps demonstrate why families can trust you with the care of their loved one. They also have a blog section, which is a fun way to provide extra insight and information to someone hunting for their perfect home!

https://www.justlikehomellc.com – This website is really fun in many ways! To start, the logo is pink, which is rarely used by companies for their marketing. I think it's a perfect choice for two reasons: this is a woman-owned business, and 75% of seniors living in assisted living homes are female. As you already know, Daughter Judy is doing the shopping for the home, and this could be that one small subconscious feature that sets Deirdre's home apart. Other awesome choices include putting her caregiver ratio right at the top, including a pop-up to schedule a tour, and posting lots of real-life videos and photos. But all the way at the bottom, she did something really special. She posted and created a ton of content videos explaining all about RAL, such as why someone should choose a smaller home and how to connect with seniors and caregivers. She also has a link to her book, demonstrating that she is an expert on the topic. Overall, her website says, "I care. I am educated. I am well-informed. I am female-friendly." For those reasons, this page makes a great website!

FACEBOOK

Facebook is the beast that none of us want to use, but we all have to. The demographics you are targeting are not on TikTok or Twitter. Daughter Judy is 50 to 70 years old, so more than likely, she is on Facebook. Having a page with reviews, likes, and follows matters. One of our star students, Eddy, always posts fun things that he and the seniors are doing within the homes, and it's a blast to follow their page. Another student posted a picture of an adorable feeder trough that they filled with water and fish so the seniors could go fishing. How precious and fun! Things like this will attract people to your RAL, and poof, you have home tours based on your Facebook page. Most importantly, don't just create it and let it sit. Be active on it!

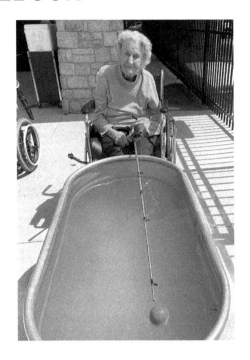

BROCHURES AND FLYERS

Brochures and flyers may seem outdated, but think about the impression you want to make and what your competitors are doing. When Daughter Judy goes to visit the big-box facility, they give her a beautiful brochure with all the features and amenities and things for her to think about when she gets home. You need to keep up with the big-box facilities and give her something physical that reminds her of the visit to your home. A clean, beautiful brochure with detailed information will do the trick. You could attach a bag of chocolate chip cookies or a customized item with your logo on it, something that makes her remember and wants to come back to you. The touring process can be overwhelming, so take-home items can be the small thing that draws them towards choosing your home. The thoughtfulness goes a long way.

Printed materials are also helpful for on-the-road marketing. If you ever visit a person or a business who may be willing to promote your home, you need to leave them with something to do that. Brochures and flyers are perfect for that type of marketing.

COMMUNITY RELATIONSHIPS

Befriending key people in your community is going to be one of the most important things you can do for your home. One of our students, Dale, took this to another level. He went home to Oklahoma and contacted every elder law attorney, long-term care insurance provider, and realtor who specialized in helping seniors move and started making friends. He always brought value first and never lost sight of how he could help or support them. Needless to say, Dale has never needed to pay very much in marketing dollars because he let his relationships do the marketing for him. This could be your winning ticket to filling your beds, too!

RAL HOME LOCATOR

When you are marketing your home, make sure to sign up for RALHome-eLocator.com and give your home a good designation on the map. This is a great place for people to search for the best-of-the-best homes in their area. The promotion and eyes on your home could be a game-changer for getting new residents to come tour your house!

BUSINESS CARDS

Business cards are still a staple in marketing. Make sure the contact information is large enough to read, keep the design clean and simple, and include a link or QR code to the home's website. Pass them out whenever the opportunity strikes!

DRIVE-BY MARKETING

Signs, banners, and flags in front of your home are a surefire way to get extra eyes on your property. If it is not allowed in your area, put it up anyways. When they tell you to take it down, oblige them, but in the meantime, enjoy the free marketing!

PLACEMENT AGENCY RELATIONSHIPS

Making connections with local placement agents will be very important. I don't want you to rely 100 percent on this to fill your beds, but having some local placement agents in your corner will help you fill beds throughout the year. I recommend avoiding companies like A Place For Mom as a national placement agency. They take a lot from you as a placement fee and it's not worth it in the long run.

You can find placement agents in your area by searching online, asking other care homeowners, and seeking out geriatric doctors and nurses and asking for recommendations. In certain markets, like Arizona, there are hundreds of placement agents to choose from, while in other markets, like Arkansas, there may not be as many. Find what you can and always keep your eye out for more options. Also, stay in touch with the agents even when your beds are full. One of our students, Carol, owns in Montana and makes it a point to send out biweekly updates on their homes to all the local placement agents, even when their beds are full. When an agent places someone in the home, Carol sends small monthly updates on the resident and how they're doing and enjoying their stay. This helps the agent feel good for having placed a person in a happy home. It also prevents agents from having the perception that you only stay in contact when you need something from them. You want to make sure to keep that connection strong at all times.

GREAT REPUTATION

Your reputation can be a great marketing tool! When your residents and their families are happy, they will be proud to share the good news with others. They will tell other people about how your home is a high-quality property where seniors are well taken care of. Having a strong reputation with local authorities can be very powerful, too. Firefighters, EMTs, and other emergency professionals have seen the inside of many senior care homes. If they say your home was well kept, clean and everyone was being loved on and cared for properly, that says a lot. So, if an ambulance is ever called to your home, make sure to impress them even in a dire situation.

TESTIMONIALS

Testimonials are vital to any and every business. Once you have some residents in the home whose families are having good experiences, capture that! Ask them to leave you a review and offer to give them $500 off the following month's rent if they bring in a referral. People want to know what other people think, so this can really help push your business to the next level! When we have asked our family members to leave a review on our Facebook page, we have been upfront and said, "We know you enjoy having your mother living in our home, and we are hoping other families will be able to enjoy the same comfort and care that you all have received over the years. Our Facebook page is new and the marketing is a little weak, so if you would be so kind as to help us out and leave a quick review of your honest feelings and opinions on the home and the care, that would be amazing. Here is the link."

Marketing can be the deciding factor in separating people who succeed from those who don't succeed in any business, but particularly this one. These 10 proven strategies will set you on the path to success in marketing your own RAL home!

CHAPTER 19
Family Issues

When it comes to Daughter Judy, that name we affectionately call the adult child who is typically responsible for the senior's care, there can be a lot to consider. For starters, the emotions involved during this time of life are at an absolute peak. There are so many changes going on that are out of everyone's control. Daughter Judy is being pulled in many directions. She is genuinely trying to do the best she can to support everyone. Typically, we see her being pulled by the needs of her elderly loved one, the cost of care, the stress of what to do with their home and items, her own family's needs (especially if she has younger children), and her job. At some point, she is just stretched too thin. We rarely, if ever, see a Daughter Judy who comes in cool, calm, and collected. Instead, they are usually some combination of stressed to the max, scared, guilty, unsure, irritable, indecisive, angry, worried, and overbearing.

When Daughter Judy calls your home to ask questions, remember the emotionality surrounding this call. Remember the fear, the guilt, the worry. Try to get to the core of her questions. What is really worrying her about this choice, and where is the fear coming from? Reflect her concerns and explain how your home may be able to address those concerns. Do not just launch into explaining how you've renovated the home and how you painted it all baby blue or how you filled in the pool and put in a rose garden. Listen to what Daughter Judy is worried about. If she mentions healthy food for her dad, then focus on your private chef and made-to-order meals. Mention how your menu is doctor- and state-approved, and ask what her dad's favorite meal is. Let her know you're happy to incorporate his favorite meal into the weekly schedule so he feels comfortable. Let her know she's welcome to come by and join for the meals throughout the week, whenever she would like. Don't focus on the size of the bedroom if she's worried about the food. If she says her dad is fussy about his haircut and is worried that she won't be able to pick him up every week to take him to the barber, let her know you have a hairdresser who comes in each week at no extra cost. It's important to you, too, that he feels handsome and fresh. She will be grateful that you get it, that you understand those fears and worries, and that you have a solution ready for her. Don't forget, above all else, the most important advice is to LISTEN to Daughter Judy.

Something else to consider when it comes to Daughter Judy is that she may be an adult child taking the lead on finding a home for her parent, but more than likely, there are multiple children involved. Most of these seniors have many children, and some of them will criticize the way Daughter Judy is choosing to care for Mom or Dad. This can cause extra strain. We often see families where the other siblings are not accepting of the choices she is making and are constantly telling her what she is doing wrong or what they think she should be doing. The main thing to remember is that Daughter Judy is the one making the decisions. She is in charge. Only Daughter Judy is having conversations with doctors, nurses, insurance, homes, etc., and because she has this responsibility, she also has earned the power to make the choice. This can be a very strained time in her life, and it's important to let her know that you are thankful for the effort she's putting into Mom or Dad's care. Tell her that she is doing a great job and that even if no one is saying thank you, because it is a thankless job, she is doing amazing. This is the senior care industry; hugs and words of gratitude are welcome, and they go a long way! Daughter Judy needs support, and you can be both a care homeowner and a friend.

Sometimes a Daughter Judy visits your home, and you realize that they are not a good fit for your community. More often than not, it isn't the senior who isn't the right fit; it's the family. Many seniors blend into the community well, but occasionally, a family can be a bit much. My dad dealt with a family like this in one of his homes. There were no issues at all with the senior, who was sweet and lovely, but the family… oh lord! The family would visit three times a week and would bring 12-plus people to the house. They would bring a bunch of groceries, kick the chef out, and start cooking in the kitchen. They were loud and vulgar, screaming obscenities and offending everyone else in the house and making it a very uncomfortable environment. The staff were at a loss for how to control this behavior. When they asked the family members to not curse while in the house, the family would become even louder and more obnoxious. When the manager was called in to handle the situation, she offered for the family to bring homecooked meals for their senior but asked them to please not dismiss the chef because it was not safe for them to be making the food for everyone inside the home without a food-handler license. The family got heated with this accusation, yelled at the manager, and continued to do what they wanted to do.

Situations like this kept arising, and finally, my father was called in to help. He was a very hands-off owner, and staff were typically able to handle issues on their own. With this family, though, it had gotten to the point where the caregivers and manager felt it was necessary to remove this senior from the home because of the family's disruptiveness and disrespect. My father invited the family to sit down with him and the manager. He and his manager explained to the family how their behaviors were negatively impacting residents and staff. They reassured the family there was no issue with the senior, and the senior was welcome to stay, but they also made it clear that the family's conduct was not welcome and would not be tolerated. The family became enraged. So, my father told the family that they had 24 hours to remove the senior and their belongings from the home, provided a list of other homes in the area, and sent the dismissal letter home with them that night. The following day, they came to get their loved one and moved them into a new home. Problem solved.

Now, this scenario wasn't necessarily an issue with Daughter Judy. Just the one Daughter Judy did the home tour and made the decision, and there was really no issue with her in the beginning and no indication that the family would be this much of a disaster. Because the residents and their families are signing residency agreements rather than tenant/landlord agreements, you are able to remove residents at any time for any reason.

You are not locked in and do not have to keep residents if they or their family are not a good fit or if your services are no longer a good match for their care needs. It's important to make sure your residency agreement outlines your expectations, including a behavior clause for both the family and the resident. If we didn't have that clause in our contracts with that family, it would have been more difficult to cut ties with them. Those little tips and tricks are what could save you from big drama!

You can help Daughter Judy in many ways. First, overcommunicate. It is so important to make her feel at ease with this decision. You want to be understanding, to be sympathetic to her worries and guilt. You want to give her all the news and feedback that you can to help her sleep at night. She may be one of your greatest marketing tools and referral sources, so make sure that you are appeasing her needs appropriately. Usually, throughout the first month, I send a photo of the senior doing something exciting that I know will bring peace to Daughter Judy. Sharing photos, sending text messages, writing monthly newsletters, or posting on Facebook will help alleviate stress and instill a sense of comfort.

We had a resident named Solomon, and his son was so worried about him moving into our home. Solomon loved to listen to opera music and read books, so on day one of his stay in our home, we played lots of opera music for him. I sent a video to his son of him listening to the music and swinging his arms along with the rhythm. He was smiling and enjoying himself. Then, three days later, I caught Solomon reading a book with a caregiver in a sunny corner outside under one of our lemon trees, so I sent a picture to his son. Both of these little things made a world of difference. He was so thankful and grateful to have his dad in a home that listened and cared about his needs.

Second, go above and beyond! You can do this in so many different ways. You could find out each resident's favorite foods and add them to the menu when they move in. You could also work with different activity programs to find what your seniors like the most. If you have a musical bunch, add in activities like karaoke and Broadway sing-along days or invite a local choir group to come sing to your residents. If they are into gardening, add a tower garden or aboveground planters where they can do fun projects like painting flowerpots and planting seeds.

There are some incredible resources in our industry, such as programs where you can record a senior's story in writing, on camera, or in audio recordings. We have done beautiful sit-down interviews where we ask the seniors all about their lives, their past loves, their children, where they grew up, their parents and siblings, the good times and the bad. The seniors light up at the opportunity to share about their lives. It's a gorgeous and unforgettable gift to give to the families once the senior moves on. Those moments and memories will set your home apart, and the families will be forever grateful to you.

Third, you can refer Daughter Judy to other services that can help her. For example, Mom's House is an organization that helps with cleaning out seniors' homes before they sell. It can be a very overwhelming process without help. When you have a company who comes in, sits down with you, understands that stress, and says, "Don't worry we've got this," it gives Daughter Judy the chance to take a deep breath. Mom's House trains people in certain regions to be Senior Transition Specialists so they can properly handle all of these tasks and then help the adult children with finding a great home for their loved one. If you befriend the Senior Transition Specialist in your area, they may be a great referral source for you! www.momshouse.com/ral

Finally, be honest. Daughter Judy may come in not knowing exactly what their parent or loved one needs and what their capabilities are. Throughout their stay in your home, you may discover that their needs are far beyond what you initially were told. It's important to have that crucial conversation with Daughter Judy. She needs to know what is really going on. If Mom or Dad has incontinence or is very angry when we try to change their clothes or is up all night or curses at any of the caregivers who are from another country, it's important to share that as empathetically as possible with Daughter Judy.

The last thing you want is for her to not be in the loop on what's really happening, and then something bad happens, and now she is in shock because she doesn't understand how that could have even possibly happened! If she is in the loop and you are able to communicate the truth of the matter with her, she will be much more understanding and open to the care you are able to provide and the struggles you are facing. I would always rather let the adult children know upfront about any issues we may be having within the home and let them make the decisions on how we can help with tailoring their care plan to address the issue.

CHAPTER 20

Highs and Lows

Even when you're doing everything right as an RAL owner, there will be highs and lows working in this industry. You will experience highs when your beds are full, your staff is happy, and you have incredible residents who are thriving. Lows happen when one or more of your residents passes, you're not 100 percent full, or you have an issue with staff or one of the family members. No matter the obstacles that come your way, you will be able to take them in stride if you stay connected with your passion, grit, and why.

One of our students, Kevin, went through a low time that stands out in my memory. Around January and February, after the excitement of the holidays, some residents pass. It's something about accomplishing that date, being there for the holiday, or seeing that family member one more time, and then they feel ready to move on to the next life. That sounds strange, but there's really no other way to explain it. Well, around this time of year, Kevin lost four of his 12 residents in a three-week time span. It was tough on a personal and emotional level, and it was also tough from a business standpoint. The reality of being a business owner is that the beds need to be filled. Kevin immediately used his resources and scheduled a call with our team, and we walked him through the next steps. He began by calling the local placement agents, bumping up his online ad budgets, and chatting with neighbors and others in the area, like geriatric doctors and nurses, hospice care, and elder law attorneys. Within 10 days, those four beds were filled. It was incredible. There is always a high on the other side of a low if you're willing to put in the work, and Kevin was! We were so proud of him stepping up in a difficult time.

Many people aren't prepared for the emotionality in this industry. The lows of losing a resident who meant a lot to you, the caregivers, and the other residents is tough. Even if someone is 95 and needs help with most of their activities of daily living (ADLs), it's never easy to lose someone. In our industry, there are really only three ways you're leaving our homes. First, a resident may need elevated care that we cannot help with, so a nursing home is the next step. Second, the family or resident is no longer a good fit and needs to move to another facility or home. Third, the resident passes on. About 85 percent of the time, our residents stay in the home until they pass. Knowing that this is someone's last stop before passing makes the moments you spend with them even more special. I remember hearing a quote when my grandfather passed, and it's true for our industry as well: "If it hurts to lose them, it means the love and the connection meant something. It means it was real." I like to think that every time a resident passes, I'm blessed to have been a small part of their journey in this beautiful life, and that means a lot. It's a way to give back that is truly from the heart.

Of course, there are plenty of highs that come with being a care home-owner, like the praise and gratitude you receive from the families and the deep connections you, your team, and your residents form. Our student, Joe, is a tough guy from Boston who become such a softie for his residents and their families. He and his wife came to our RAL National Convention one year, and she shared with me how being a part of this industry completely changed him and how thankful she was to see this gentler side of him. Another student, Darlene, owned a home in North Carolina where one of her resident's son would visit every Friday. Over the years his dad lived in the home, the son made friends with the other residents, so even after his dad passed, he continued to visit on Fridays to see the other residents and spend time with them. Darlene welcomed him with open arms every Friday. That's the love, kindness, and respect you see when you have a smaller community, a family environment, and a truly loving and welcoming care home.

PART 5

The Future

CHAPTER 21

What Is RAL Academy?

At Residential Assisted Living Academy, we teach you the good, the bad, and the ugly of assisted living. We show you in-depth how to find the home, how to fund the home, and how to fill the home. It's an all-encompassing training unlike anything else offered in the market. As the population ages and more people require assisted living, there will also be more people getting into this industry, but we are the only family-owned national company who has taught thousands of people nationwide how to be successful in this incredible industry.

WHAT WE DO AND DO NOT TEACH

In our training, we take you behind the scenes. We welcome you on live tours of our homes and our most successful students' homes. We show you what to look for and what to avoid when searching for the right property. We go over business valuations if you want to purchase an existing home, and floor plans if you're building from the ground up. We teach you how to work with placement agents, local community members, and administrators to have the best relationships. We show you how to do your demographic research and determine if a market is good or bad and if you should stay with it or look elsewhere. We teach you what to look for in your staff, specifically your managers and caregivers. We share how to host home tours and what to say or not say. We also have an entire memory care section if that is the route you are interested in taking.

We fill you with motivation and inspiration to change the world through assisted living. We give you resources that you cannot find elsewhere and connections that are only available to our students. We provide you with memberships to the RAL National Association and offer many opportunities to access free or discounted programs that will guide you in your business creation and expansion with your very own care home.

It is equally important to point out what we are NOT teaching. We are not teaching you how to become a caregiver or administrator. We are not licensing you to become someone who is going to work inside the home. We are not teaching you the day-by-day ins and outs of the home life as an administrator. Although we do have some doctors and nurses on the team, we are not teaching anything related to the medical profession.

We are focused on how to invest from an entrepreneurial perspective and how to operate the business at large. All of our experts on stage are past students who came to the training, learned everything they could, went back into the world, created their own care homes, and now are back to teach you even more. That's what we are all about: giving back and sharing the message of doing good and doing well!

WHY WE TEACH

One of my favorite questions is, "If this industry is so amazing and you're making so much money, why not keep it a secret, corner the market, and own this niche? Why do you teach others how to do this?"

Here's the thing: even if I created 100 of these Residential Assisted Living care homes, it still wouldn't be enough to solve this crisis. If I truly care about seniors and what's to come for them, the best thing I can do is use my God-given skills to share this message and get other people on board with helping open more and more quality care homes. If we all work together, we may actually be able to make a difference. If I go at it alone, first, it would be selfish, and second, it wouldn't actually be helping. There's enough pie for everyone.

I love to teach investors and entrepreneurs how to own and operate Residential Assisted Living homes because this is my life's mission. My father spent the final 10 years of his life learning, growing, and investing into this industry, becoming the "Godfather of Assisted Living" and really teaching everyone and anyone he could how to impact and make a difference within the senior care industry.

If I let that legacy die with him, I wouldn't be honoring him and his life's work. He found nothing more incredible than the impact this industry made on people. It was so beautiful to watch his whole life soften and sweeten and to be able to share that with others from across the world. We started something so incredible together, and I don't want that to stop!

When we get to share the message of doing good and doing well, we bring a little more light back into the world. We give Daughter Judy hope. We give investors who are burnt out on single-family rentals or fix-and-flips a reason to walk away and start something bigger and greater than themselves. We give families relief, restful nights, and hope. We give an industry with a terrible reputation some hope and light. All of those things make a difference to me. They encourage me to wake up each morning and continue this impactful contribution Residential Assisted Living Academy has on the world. I can't help but smile when I see it click in someone's eyes or when an entrepreneur says to me, "This checks my boxes." It's all worth it, and it all matters in the end. It means the world to me to carry my father's legacy forward and to live this legacy until my last breath.

WHY COME TO RAL ACADEMY

If you are someone who is ready to make a difference in your life and the lives of those around you, someone who wants to make a mark on the world and change their community, then coming to our training would be your next best step. In our course, we have people from all walks of life: investors, entrepreneurs, medical professionals, stay-at-home moms, engineers, farmers—you name it. Because this is not a one-size-fits-all industry, it's welcoming to anyone who wants to join, as long as you have the right heart and you care about doing quality work with the creation of your new RAL home.

If you are someone who is ready to cash flow over $10,000 each month on one single-family home, who understands that with great reward comes great work, who has the grit, passion, and determination it will take, then this may be the right course for you. It's not going to be easy, but it's going to be worth it. When something's worth it, you'll do whatever it takes to get it done. If that rings true in your heart with your past commitments, then Residential Assisted Living Academy opens its doors to you. We are here to make a mark on the world, and we can't do it alone. We need as many people as possible to create quality, beautiful care homes where our seniors can live out their last years of life in safe, loving, and caring hands. The numbers don't lie, and neither do we; it's time to take action!

My father's life mission was to positively impact *one* million people through Residential Assisted Living, and Residential Assisted Living Academy is blessed to be able to continue doing that work. But we can't go at it alone. I hope you can join us at our next training event. You can find more information at www.ralacademy.com/events. If you are interested in taking a deeper dive into what the Residential Assisted Living Academy offers, we have free webinars and informational discovery calls available at www.ral101.com.

CHAPTER 22

What Is the Future of RAL?

When we look into the future of RAL Academy and the Residential Assisted Living industry in general, I see lots of bright, shiny prospects ahead. First, we are not even at the peak of need for these homes and beds, so I see massive financial opportunities to be had no matter what role you want to play. You could get into the medical bed field or the long-term care insurance game or the sale and organization of seniors' homes. The opportunities are endless! At the end of the day, it's important to be in the right place at the right time. It's so clear what is to come and how we can be involved. It's time for you to create that personal and business vision and see how they match up with your WHY. It's time for you to decide how you want to ride the wave!

My personal vision for RAL has much more to do with how many people we can get involved in this movement. We don't have to settle for the status quo. Gone are the days of only having taxi cabs or a ride from a friend now that Uber exists, or the days of only hotels or bed-and-breakfasts now that Airbnbs exist. We are disrupting the industry; it is no longer only "big-box" facilities or unaffordable in-home care. You've taken the red pill, you've seen the light, and you know what is on the other side. Residential Assisted Living is the other option. It's the disruptor. It's the future! My personal vision is to expose as many people as possible to this newly realized type of care, to share the message of doing good and doing well, and to give entrepreneurs and investors alike a creative solution for their loved one's care, their own care, and leaving a legacy for their heirs or children.

I am living my father's dream, his vision, his legacy. He created our companies because his passion burned deeply. My life changed forever when I left my airline career to join him in building a family business. It is now my job to carry this vision forward. If I let the good news die with me, if I stop teaching others how to become financially free from one single-family home being used for Residential Assisted Living, it would be wrong, selfish, and absolutely cruel of me! It's so utterly important for me to keep this company and this concept afloat. I must do this to honor my father. He didn't become the Godfather of Assisted Living overnight. His hard work and determination got him where he was, and I am blessed to have been along for the ride. Now it's my mission to give back to as many others as I can. If you're not living a legacy, then how can you leave a legacy?

Myles Munroe, a prolific Bahamian pastor who passed away in 2014, once said, "True leaders don't invest in buildings. Jesus never built a building. They invest in people. Why? Because success without a successor is failure. So, your legacy should not be in buildings, programs, or projects; your legacy must be in people." Sometimes people think that my father's legacy was building and creating RAL care homes, but it's not. It's so much more than that. His legacy is about a mission to help change an industry that so desperately needs help. His legacy is about changing the lives of families from the inside out. His legacy is about making an impact and proving that just because things have been done a certain way, we don't have to carry on doing them that way. His legacy is everlasting because it's about the people. It's about the mission. It's about something so much bigger than all of us.

When my dad came up with the motto "Do Good and Do Well," he wanted to make sure he was attracting the right people: people who had a calling to make a difference, people who would be dedicated to this mission, people who weren't just about cash-flowing like crazy! And then he added the mission statement of "positively impacting one million people through Residential Assisted Living." One home doesn't just positively impact those 10 seniors living inside of it. It also positively impacts the caregivers who have a better place to work and are treated with respect. It positively impacts the seniors' families, relieving them from guilt and anger and preventing the abuse that happens in in larger facilities. It gives them a chance to have their lives back. Daughter Judy matters to her family. When she gives up everything to take care of Mom or Dad, her personal life suffers. Opening a Residential Assisted Living care home gives her life back! She can be a mom again. She can go to soccer games and dance recitals and debates and spend those life-changing moments with her kids. She can be a wife again and be present, focused, and open in her marriage. The entire family is affected when Mom or Dad find peaceful living in a Residential Assisted Living care home. Not to mention the seniors themselves. They do not want to burden their families, but they need the care. They are positively impacted by living in these homes because they can also let go of the anger or guilt. They can enjoy peace and tranquility in their final years of life.

All anyone wants in life is to love and be loved. Owning and operating a Residential Assisted Living home gives you that chance, and to be frank, it's kind of magical. The feel-good side of this industry, the total life-changing impact you can have on families and their loved ones, it really makes you want to create more and more and more of these incredible homes.

As far as legacy goes, it may seem from the outside that it's about creating businesses or buildings and passing those cash cows down, but from the inside, it's about changing lives and passing down the opportunity to impact far beyond your true reach. I am honored and blessed that Gene Guarino, the Godfather of Assisted Living, was my father. He was a sympathetic, kind-hearted, and genuine man who built some incredible businesses and left an indelible mark on this world. It is my honor to carry on his legacy and share his mission with the world.

I want nothing more than to be able to give back to my future children in the same way my father gave to me. He sacrificed in more ways than one to provide for us. After years of investing in so many other real estate avenues, he stumbled into Residential Assisted Living out of need and desperation, just like many of you may be feeling. When our whole world came crashing down and we had to find a home for my grandmother, that's when we discovered Residential Assisted Living. It started as a solution to a problem, then it became a passion, and then we created a mission and changed others' lives along the way. When I hear stories from our students, I know I am doing something good in this world. On the opposing end, when I hear the hate of people on social media, those keyboard warriors telling me I'm taking advantage of old people, it fuels my fire even more. You see, it couldn't be further from the truth. All I want to do is help you and others like you to be exposed to other opportunities for cash flow, for care for a loved one, for leaving your own legacy. It stems from our mission of positively impacting one million people through Residential Assisted Living. I personally cannot do that alone. I need help. This book is a start, but we need you to go out into the world and share the "do good, do well" message. Come to our class and learn how to create your own Residential Assisted Living home. Let's do this together.

CHAPTER 23

So Now What?

After reading this book, you may be thinking, "Well, what next?!" Are you ready to jump in? If so, a 3-Day Fast Track training might be the next best step for you. You can find more information on those courses at www.ralacademy.com/events.

Maybe you're a go-at-your-own-pace type of learner, and doing something from home suits your personal needs. If so, the online Home Study Course is a great choice, and you can find more information at www.ralhsc.com.

Or maybe you need to really dig deep and talk with someone from our staff. If so, check out www.ral101.com to schedule a call, watch a free webinar, or download some mini courses.

Lastly, if you are looking for a home for a loved one, check out www.ral-homelocator.com for the best-of-the-best care homes across the country!

And if you are already an owner/operator of a Residential Assisted Living home, please join our membership at www.RALNationalAssociation.org for free webinars, discounts, and major member benefits like legal updates, continuing education courses, surveys, and more!

If you are interested in some of our other resources like our blogs and articles, head to www.residentialassistedlivingacademy.com/blog. For featured podcasts and episodes, go to www.residentialassistedlivingacademy.com/podcast-appearances/.

We also have a great time on social media posting fun, informative videos on our Instagram at www.instagram.com/ralacademy/ and more recently on our TikTok page www.tiktok.com/@ral.academy. You can find us anywhere really!

YouTube: https://www.youtube.com/c/ResidentialAssistedLivingAcademy

Facebook: https://www.facebook.com/ResidentialAssistedLivingAcademy/

LinkedIn: https://www.linkedin.com/company/residential-assisted-living-academy

Twitter: https://twitter.com/RALAcademy

We are so passionate about what we do and hope that you too will soon be on board with the mission of Doing Good and Doing Well! I hope that these stories, lessons, and tips are helpful to you. I hope that this book brings you faith that there are still good people in this world trying to change things that have always been done a certain way. I hope that you get a glimpse inside of an ever-changing and exciting industry. Like my dad always said, "You're going to get involved in Assisted Living one way or another: either you or a loved one will be living in the home, writing a check to someone to take care of you. Or you could own the business, live for free, and pass a cash-flowing blessing onto your family when you pass on."

It's up to you to choose how you get involved from here. You could invest in someone else's project and be a JV lender or private investor. You could own the real estate and lease it to someone to use your home for this project. You could own the real estate and business. My wish is that you determine what role you want to play and that you let this book guide you to that next step in your journey. Let it point to where you may be able to impact your community, and may you seek out those opportunities that lie in front of you. I hope that you help carry my father's vision and legacy forward.

I wish for all seniors to have access to quality care in incredible homes with the best food, love, and service. I hope for entrepreneurs to see there are more opportunities than just the same old same old, and that they step outside of their comfort zone and do more. I hope you write down your why, determine your passion and commitment level, and make it count. I look forward to hopefully meeting you one day in our trainings, and I wish you all of the best of luck in your life!

"If you're going to live, leave a legacy. Make a mark on the world that can't be erased."

-Maya Angelou

Meet the Author

Isabelle is a graduate from Arizona State University, a former flight attendant and Walt Disney World intern, and now Residential Assisted Living Academy's leading lady. She has been working as the COO of the company for the last eight years, keeping everyone in line and on task. She's been featured in many magazines and articles on the topic of Senior Housing and was titled one of the "Top Influencers in Senior Housing." Isabelle also won Aging Media's "the Future Leaders of Assisted Living" award in 2020, being only one of two of under 30 to make the list. Isabelle Guarino trains and teaches entrepreneurs and investors at the Residential Assisted Living Academy. She has extensive experience in building brands, launching this company and many more into national recognition while running the day-to-day operations.

She is responsible for the creation and success of RAL National Convention, RAL National Association, Recovery Housing Academy, Pitch Masters Academy, and most of the Impact Housing Group's companies. With a background in Business Marketing and Communications to working at two Fortune 500 companies, she is a true leader in business development and operations. She is a sought-after coach and trainer for all things "RAL!"

Isabelle's goal is to carry on her father's legacy by training investors & entrepreneurs how to... "Do Good & Do Well."

CPSIA information can be obtained
at www.ICGtesting.com
Printed in the USA
BVHW011115060123
655719BV00007B/534